LIVE
Laugh
LAGOM

EMBRACING THE SWEDISH WAY
TO **BALANCE** AND **HAPPINESS**

Lola A. Åkerström

Ulysses Press

Published in the US by:
ULYSSES PRESS
PO Box 3440
Berkeley, CA 94703
www.ulyssespress.com

ISBN 978-1-61243-767-5
Library of Congress Control Number: 2017952132

Printed in the United States by United Graphics Inc.

First published in 2017 in Great Britain as *Lagom: The Swedish Secret of
Living Well* by Headline Publishing Group, a Hachette UK Company

US editor: Renee Rutledge
Interior design and Illustrations: Sinem Erkas
Cover design: Rebecca Lown

Distributed by Publishers Group West

To my darling husband and kids, who
fill my life with joy, love, and meaning.

NOTE FROM THE AUTHOR

I first noticed this unspoken ethos, like the awkward elephant in the room, years ago while dining with violinists and bassists who perform in local orchestras, including the Royal Philharmonic and Radio Symphony Orchestras in Stockholm, Sweden. A typical week for

"Where there is modesty, there is virtue."
Swedish Proverb

them could involve playing at Nobel Prize ceremonies or a more private gig for the Swedish royal family.

But I was the odd one out. The outsider who'd been invited to this rather casual dinner where the unspoken dress code was well-worn blue jeans paired with loose-fitting tops for the ladies and more tailored, tighter cuts for the men, all feet clad in warm woolen socks.

A certain air of moderation enveloped our group. The gratuitous peppering of self-achievements seemed nonexistent within our conversation. No one willingly divulged personal information unless asked by another guest. The average number of languages fluently spoken within the group was three each, yet this class of globetrotters who'd traversed the world multiple times quickly dismissed their skills because they weren't native speakers. On several occasions, our banter dipped into long stretches of silence, one which seemed perfectly comfortable for them. The small apartment we inhabited oozed warmth and contentment.

That subconscious moment was when *lagom* as a quiet rule began to clearly emerge from the shadows for me as a new resident in Sweden. Still, I threw it all down to modesty and humility among fast friends who knew each other well and didn't feel the need to brag or take up the entire conversation.

But that silent ethos raised its head once again in a completely different setting, and that was when I realized it was also a shape-shifting public code of conduct along the lines of "appropriate."

I noticed it when our group of passengers arriving in Stockholm from Swedish Lapland waited in silence at a baggage conveyor belt for delayed luggage. Beyond acquaintances sharing words among themselves, strangers didn't interact with each other for close to thirty minutes during that unusually long technical delay. Had I been somewhere else, I'd have nudged a fellow passenger, and we would have commiserated as loudly as we could about our predicament.

But here, within the ecosystem of the Swedish mindset, stating the obvious seemed unnecessary.

This ideology was further solidified when I was running late for a Swedish class and had prepared an explanation for my tardiness to deliver to my teacher.

"No need," a local promptly advised me. "No need to explain yourself. Just apologize for being late." I didn't need to share more information than was necessary.

Especially if I wasn't asked.

"Give equal in reply, answer according to the call."
Swedish Proverb

That moment brought me full circle back to my dinner with the musicians, and I could see that principle in all its clarity now. Over time, what started out as the awkward elephant in the room morphed into an unseen guiding spirit whispering reminders into one's ear.

"Not too much, not too little," it whispers. "Just right."

Not the middle. Not average. Not complacency. Just right.

And that distinction remains the underlying power of lagom as the basis for achieving an optimal lifestyle where one gives and receives in equal part without disturbing the balance between individuality and group dynamics.

I'd heard of this unspoken custom long before moving to Sweden, and over time, I've come to adopt lagom in various aspects of my own life as I've further immersed myself in Swedish culture. This book deeply reflects my unique vantage point—a marriage between the objectivity that comes with looking in and the subjectivity that comes with an intimate and multifaceted relationship with Sweden.

Lagom is so much more than the simple act of moderation it is so commonly associated with.

And through this book, I hope to show you how this little, understated word not only deeply permeates the Swedish psyche (including through old Swedish proverbs), but how it may very well be the little secret that could push you toward living your most sustainable life yet.

Not just living a life of balance, but finding the perfect equilibrium for you.

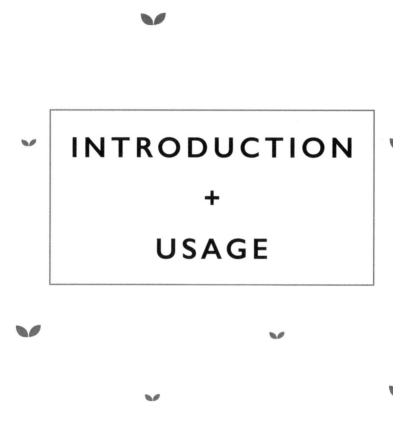

INTRODUCTION
+
USAGE

"The right amount is best."

Swedish Proverb

We live in times of undue pressure that demand we constantly remain plugged in and connected with the rest of the world, stay on top of breaking news by the second, and keep up with the dizzying speed of technological advancements, lifestyle changes, and pop culture norms.

We move at an unnatural pace trying to keep up with others, stay relevant, and avoid getting metaphorically left behind. We continually feel the internal push against external pressures from our surroundings—from work, play, relationships, and society. We constantly derail our own natural tracks in life and are sometimes forced to push our individual reset buttons.

So we disconnect, detox, and shut the world out in an effort to relax, recuperate, and rejuvenate our bodies emotionally, mentally, and physically. These solutions, no matter how revitalizing they are at the precise moments we activate them, are often temporary. So in our continued quest to find new ways of balancing our lives and inching closer to our happy mediums, we often look outside our boxes of comfort to draw inspiration and learn from others.

What are others around the world doing well that we can emulate? What are they doing poorly that we can avoid?

While the Swedish word lagom has recently emerged as a new lifestyle trend to consider adopting into everyday living, this isn't the first time we've borrowed foreign words from other cultures as daily inspiration to center us and get us back on our individual paths.

Hakuna matata means "no worries" in Swahili. This perspective-giving word means we need to invite more calm into our lives by breaking out of our uptight shells. It doesn't mean taking a carefree attitude toward every situation, but rather stepping back so as to look at the bigger picture with clarity and to avoid making mountains out of molehills.

Carpe diem, which is Latin for "seize the day," implores us to grab opportunities as they come and take advantage of today because tomorrow may never come. The future is not guaranteed to us and we should fill the day with meaningful experiences.

The German word *fernweh* denotes wanderlust and a craving for travel. It is the constant need to be somewhere new, different, and distant from the familiar, a pull that drags us to explore the unfamiliar.

Our Danish cousins have given us *hygge,* which, on the surface, encompasses coziness, intimacy, and relaxation with our loved ones, as well as with ourselves, but on a deeper level denotes an emotional state of contentment and happiness at specific moments in time.

Now the Swedes have loaned us the word lagom.

This term is the fundamental key to unlocking the very mindset of Nordic culture. Lagom is not just a word but the very essence of what it means to be a Swede and live like one. It is the secret that holds the explanation to the Swedish lifestyle of social consciousness, moderation, and sustainability.

But like the other borrowed expressions above, how can lagom fit into our own lives, and what does it aim to teach us about ourselves?

Over centuries, why have Swedes proclaimed "Lagom is best," as the old proverb says?

And what does lagom truly mean?

DEFINING THE UNDEFINABLE

First, we need to learn how to properly say the word.

Lagom is often written as "lar-gohm," where the "lar" sounds like "bar." However, the closest articulation of lagom for an English speaker phonetically is "laaaw-gum." That is, drawing out the word "law" with a soft emphasis on the "w" so you'll purse your lips the same way a native Swedish speaker would.

Secondly, lagom has no precise definition. Rather, a series of explanations and loose translations try to demystify this very Swedish word.

On the surface, it is often defined as "just the right amount" and "everything in moderation," which carry an air of appropriateness. That is further filtered down to mean that there is no need for excess, exaggerations, unnecessary public displays, and unwarranted showiness.

If you open up an English thesaurus, other synonyms you will readily pull out include just enough, in moderation, appropriate, the right amount, just right, sufficient, fitting, suitable, equilibrium, balance, golden mean, the happy medium, fit, apt, proper, precise, reasonable, and harmony.

But lagom is so much more than a predefined box of synonyms that mean moderation. In its most powerful form, lagom denotes something that is as close to contextual perfection and satisfaction as you can get.

Lagom doesn't literally mean perfection, which in itself is unachievable, it means the optimal solution, the most harmonious wavelength at which you can and should operate. It exemplifies a subconscious utopia where the specific choice you make regarding a situation, a moment, an interaction, is the best choice for you as an individual or for the groups in which you find yourself.

Boiling down the true essence of lagom to its very core, it means striving for the ultimate balance in life that, when applied to all aspects of your existence, can help guide you toward operating at your most natural, effortless state.

Consider the heroine of British author Robert Southey's 1837 children's fairytale, *Goldilocks and the Three Bears*, on her quest to find the chair, bowl of porridge, and bed that were "just right" for her. Papa Bear's bowl of porridge was probably lagom for him. As was Mama Bear's own bowl. We never really consider this but rather are steered toward Goldilocks's own perfect portion.

The state and measurement of lagom means different things to different folk. My satisfaction may vary from yours but we can both be satisfied.

Lagom represents the ultimate sweet spot or golden mean in your own life, and more importantly, encourages you to fully operate within the sweet spot that's just right for you.

HOW LAGOM IS USED IN EVERYDAY LANGUAGE

While lagom underpins the Swedish mentality, it is also more commonly used as either an adverb or an adjective, and very rarely in its noun or substantive form, *lagomet,* which means "the balance" or "the equilibrium."

Using the word in a sentence transforms how we are expected to process that sentence. The presence of the word lagom within a conversation immediately signals to the listener that whatever contextual situation the speaker is referencing needs to be processed along the lines of "optimal" or "just right."

Meaning, in describing something to you as lagom, my idea of the "perfect" lagom state may not necessarily equate to the exact same lagom state for you. Yet, the presence of the word in my sentence instantly connects both our ideals of what lagom means, and you move into that mental space of recognition.

In other words, my lagom may not be your lagom, but we're both operating at individual optimums.

And that in itself is the beautiful essence of lagom.

As an adverb

When used as an adverb, it modifies verbs, adjectives, and other adverbs, and consciously steers the listener to process conversations with measurement parameters looking for "just right."

For example:

Maten är lagom saltad—"The food is salted just right," this would mean to my taste. In your mind as the listener, you can envision the food perfectly salted to your own taste. My palate may like a saltier version than yours, but you fully understand the context.

Festen var lagom stor—"The party was the right size," meaning large enough for me to hide and resign myself to being a wallflower when needed, and small enough to feel intimate and cozy with other guests.

Det är lagom varmt ute—"It is moderately warm outside." This denotes that it is pleasant enough for me to revel in the warmth outside.

Hen kom precis lagom—"He/she came at just the right time," meaning not necessarily punctual but at the right moment.

Many of these measurements tend to address individual situations but when applied within group contexts, lagom shifts into its role of appropriate societal conduct, inviting you to balance your individual discretion within the group dynamics.

For example:

Skryt lagom!—"Don't brag like that!" Stop being such a show-off. Even if you agitated just one person, you still disturbed the entire group.

Ta en lagom portion—"Take a reasonable portion." So that others in the group can also get their fair share, take enough to sate your appetite, but use your discretion and wisdom to ensure everyone else will get a decent amount.

While this might feel like a burden to bear within a group, in due time, you can learn how much to give and how much to take, and to balance your needs with your wants.

That balancing of wants and needs is what brings you closer to personal contentment, the point which lagom actively pushes you toward.

As an adjective

When appearing as an adjective, lagom modifies nouns and pronouns by describing a particular quality of the word and pulling its quantitative optimum up to the surface. A synonym used within this context could be "fitting" or "appropriate." The speaker's state of lagom supercedes whatever the listener perceives as lagom.

For example:

Stå på lagom avstånd—"Stand at a reasonable/appropriate distance," meaning not too far that it becomes an inconvenience for you but not too close that it becomes uncomfortable.

Det är precis lagom för mig—"It is just right/enough for you," meaning it has met me at my natural state of comfort.

Min lägenhet är lagom—"My apartment/flat is adequate for me," meaning I really don't need a larger or smaller place. My flat is exactly what I need at this point in my life.

LAGOM: THE SHAPE-SHIFTER

Understanding what lagom as a word denotes and how it is commonly used is crucial because lagom also comes with shape-shifting qualities and means different things in different scenarios.

In various situations, lagom changes. Depending on the context, lagom can be emotional or apathetic. It can be qualitative or quantitative, positive or negative. It can denote irony or praise. It can mean realism, logic, and common sense.

Over the next several chapters we will explore how lagom manifests itself inside your home, within your relationships, in society, at work, and in different situations you find yourself in on a daily basis.

But the biggest takeaway should be the lessons you can learn once you see how lagom is applied in these circumstances.

How can you borrow some of those lessons to enrich and give meaning to your own life and choices in ways that make sense?

What can lagom teach you at home, work, and play?

Ultimately, the role of lagom is to guide you and give you that extra push toward finding your individual effortless balance in life by bringing down the dam of pressure and letting contentment richly flow through your life.

CULTURE
+
EMOTION

"Each person forges his own happiness."

Swedish Proverb

Did you know Sweden has a rather telling nickname?

It is sometimes called *Landet lagom* ("the Lagom Land") by Swedes because lagom has fundamentally been accepted as the way of life in the country. To live like a Swede means to adopt cultural elements of lagom in various aspects of our lives. When it comes to tempering our emotions, lagom takes on the shape of moderation without extravagance.

And to begin to understand the Swedish psyche, we need to take a closer look at the word and examine just how deeply it permeates all facets of life—from culture, fashion, and well-being to business, relationships, and society in general.

A STEP BACK IN TIME

But first, we need to understand how lagom was born, when it surfaced culturally, and when it began seeping into the Swedish mind.

In the early 1600s, the word *lag*, which means "law" as well as "team," started appearing in Swedish texts. The plural form for law at the time was *lagom*. No one can really pinpoint the exact moment lagom entered the collective Swedish consciousness, but many say its roots, anchored in community, can be traced back to the Vikings between the eighth and eleventh centuries.

Lagom has also been accepted as a shortened version of the phrase *laget om*, which literally translates to "around the team." The most popularly held belief surrounding the true origins of lagom is that this mindset of being a team player and taking your fair share was passed on from generation to generation through the Vikings. It is said that communal horns filled with mead, an alcoholic beverage made from fermented honey, were passed around as everyone gathered by fires after a hard day's pillage. Each person was supposed to sip their own share in moderation so everyone else could get a fair gulp. I imagine any Viking not adhering to that rule of conduct would meet their demise.

This is when lagom began taking on its different personas symbolizing moderation—not too much, not too little, just right.

Sweden's historically Lutheran Christian values have also added puritan layers to lagom over time to denote modesty, harmony, and treating our brothers and sisters of society fairly and equally.

Historically, this intent for fairness and equality ultimately became the core thread in Sweden's political DNA as a social welfare state where moderation, the sharing of wealth by fair taxation, and equality is legislatively enforced and promoted among citizens.

So, over time, what we witness today as the collective Swedish mindset is one of conscious mindfulness shaped by how we should exist within communities, as well as how we should live our own lives in a way that doesn't negatively impact or inconvenience others.

A LOOK AT THE PRESENT

If you asked the average Swede on the street when their country last went to war in modern history, they might respond with "Never."

With cultural roots anchored in equality and moderation, the Swedish national code of conduct is one of consensus, neutrality, and nonconfrontation.

It is often said that this perceived neutrality is why Sweden has given the world so many fine diplomats and negotiators, from businessman and humanitarian Raoul Wallenberg, who saved tens of thousands of Jews while serving as a Swedish special envoy to Budapest in the 1940s, to Swedish diplomat Dag Hammarskjöld, who was United Nations Secretary-General in the 1950s and tragically died in a plane crash en route to cease-fire negotiations.

Neutrality aside, it takes a village to build a nation, and our attitudes toward each other and the spaces we all inhabit help shape our collective quality of life.

Every year, the US-based nonprofit organization Social Progress Imperative ranks countries globally based on how they address societal needs, and Sweden consistently ranks in the top ten countries with the highest quality of life indexes.

The first measurement is how each country handles basic human needs such as medical care, sanitation, and shelter. The second is how solid its foundation of well-being is, which covers education, access to technology, and life expectancy. The third looks at what opportunities exist within its society for personal rights, freedom of choice, and tolerance.

In 2016 Sweden ranked sixth worldwide with high scores of well over ninety out of a hundred when it came to addressing basic human needs, access to knowledge and information, and environmental quality.

This mindset of equality and belief in sharing is also why Sweden regularly ranks as one of the world's most gender-egalitarian countries.

According to the 2016 *Global Gender Gap Report*, which measures gender equality across education, politics, economics, and health, Sweden ranks fourth in the world, only behind Iceland, Finland, and Norway. The shining qualities of lagom—equality, fairness, and optimality—have helped push Sweden toward the high standards of living that the country is well known for.

If lagom is the basis for the Swedish lifestyle, then there is something to be said for the power of that word and how we could benefit from adopting elements of its ideology into our own lives.

However, lagom isn't a word that is embraced by everyone. Even among Swedes.

THE SWEDISH RESTRAINT

Because lagom is measured differently by everyone, it has some qualities that some people feel impede their personal lifestyles instead of enhancing and enriching them as the word was originally intended to do.

"Better to be silent than speak ill."
Swedish Proverb

The neutrality, restraint, and conformity that stem from moderation have often been seen as an undue and rather austere burden to bear. It can stifle creativity and ambition, and this avoidance of extremes keeps us in happy bubbles of complacency and mediocrity that never challenge us to test new things, fail, and grow.

On a basic level, we see lagom as the opposite of excess. So any gesture or emotion that seems out of place within a group setting is often frowned upon...silently.

This is what I call "the Silence of the Swedes," and as the old saying goes, it is better to be silent than to speak ill, to admonish quietly rather than also fall victim to the very same act that drew one's admonition.

Many travelers to Sweden marvel at the country's physical beauty—from its lush countryside dotted with cute Monopoly-like red cottages to its capital city of Stockholm, which stunningly spreads across fourteen islands. Yet many have also come away perplexed by some of its societal rules when it comes to interacting with strangers in public spaces like buses, subways, and on the street. There is a certain quietness that is often misconstrued as indifference or outright coldness, and which could be taken personally if we end up on its receiving end.

But the thread that weaves silence around us is lagom.

Rather than being cold, apathetic, or antisocial, lagom tries to ensure that you are mindful of your neighbor. So while you as a foreigner might be aching for that local touch, interaction, and acceptance, I as a

Swede may be regarding you from a mental space of moderation and a desire to make sure you have your own space and aren't inconvenienced by my own presence.

This is why Swedes are generally not fans of random chitchat with strangers or stating the obvious, and why this is often a source of culture shock for many new residents and travelers. Conversations with friends and strangers can include long stretches of silence. This reserve is often a very comfortable space for the Swede, while it may feel like awkward torture for the stranger.

One might complain that it's often difficult to connect and build rapport with a Swede. And in a culture that doesn't go in for exaggerated gesticulation to communicate nonverbally, for a foreigner, sitting in silence with a Swede can often feel like sitting at a high-stakes card game with their poker face on. It's a trait that's more evident in certain regions of the country, such as the North.

A popular Swedish proverb says that it is better to be quiet and be perceived as less knowing than to open your mouth and remove all doubt. Because lagom ensures you only share the information that is necessary to the situation at hand, small talk may often be misconstrued as oversharing. Gratuitous compliments are rarely given because you want your actions to speak for themselves, in turn warranting praise. Criticism is invited when you do and say too much, and can be avoided by saying and doing nothing.

And so the silence continues.

MEET JANTE—
LAGOM'S JEALOUS COUSIN

Because my lagom isn't necessarily the same as your lagom, what aims to be the ultimate balance to guide us toward our individual levels of contentment can actually breed resentment, because lagom cannot be applied to everyone in equal measure.

**"Over-praise
is a burden."**
Swedish Proverb

So there is a dark underbelly to lagom within group settings that not only insists we conform, but that we also can't bring our own individual levels of lagom into the group. We can't be too much or too little of anything, and we cannot unwittingly think that we are better than others within the group.

In the 1933 novel by Danish-Norwegian author Aksel Sandemose, *A Fugitive Crosses His Tracks*, there is a fictional town called Jante where ten rules of conduct are enforced by its fictional townsfolk. Known as *jantelagen* (the Law of Jante), group mentality is governed with rules such as "You are not to think you are special" and "You are not to convince yourself that you are better than we are."

In essence, the Law of Jante not only frowns upon individual success and achievements, but also discourages individuality in favor of collective unity, suffocates ambition, and extinguishes any personal drive for more.

And so a deep-seated jealousy called *den svenska avundsjukan* (the Swedish jealousy) begins to bubble up to the surface, directed toward people we feel are successful according to our own lagom definitions of success.

If lagom is a considerate sibling, jante is that cynical cousin that tries to put us in our place. For visitors passing through the culture and being met with silence or measured responses after sharing personal achievements, it is often difficult to detect which ethos is at play.

This complex layer of jante attaching itself to lagom is why many Swedes are desperately trying to shed the stereotype. That's why Swedes you meet abroad may seem "different." They are often quick to shed lagom within groups, relationships, and situations outside of their own country. Not so much their individual operating levels of lagom, but that which is required within group settings. This is due to lagom's more negative qualities, which jante magnifies.

But make no mistake, once back in Sweden, they readily slip back into the local code of conduct.

BRINGING LAGOM BACK TO ITS CORE

Lagom was never meant to denote the word "average" or even "neutral."

Yet, over time, these words have also crept into the Swedish psyche, alongside "optimal," and continue to fuel those who feel lagom and its ideology of moderation is limiting. This also breeds some cultural misconceptions along the lines of boredom, laziness, political correctness beyond reason, and mediocrity.

However, these unattractive words don't seem to match up with the country's modernism, social progress, technological prowess, and challenging yet continued fight toward egalitarianism.

Trying to apply lagom with a broad stroke across society has to start with us as individuals, and it should be fully championed and accepted in our individual lives before we can expect lagom from others.

So if you were to take a step back and re-center lagom, you would truly understand that in its most powerful form, lagom aims to denote the contextual ideal. It tries to wrap a blanket of individual satisfaction around you, yet keeps you abreast of group dynamics and creates a sense of harmony. It tries to take you to a place of emotional maturity where whatever choice you make regarding various moments and interactions, how you choose to react or not react, is the very best choice for both you and the group.

As an unspoken guide to living your best life, lagom wants you to pause and take care of your feelings and emotions.

When referencing tangible situations, such as eating and shopping, your needs are often a lot less than what you want. When it comes to your feelings and emotions, lagom says your needs may very well exceed your wants, and that's perfectly okay. That's the space you need to operate within to get closer to your most comfortable medium and a place of harmony in your life.

You may subconsciously need an extra hug when you just wanted that initial touch. You may have wanted a lover, but truly need the support and companionship they provide beyond physical intimacy. You might want to go back to work right after a rough patch, but you may need that additional day off to take care of yourself.

What you feel you want may be a thin veil over what you really need and so fully attending to those basic needs may very well satisfy your wants and push you closer to contentment. That is what lagom, at its very core, aims to do; to make sure you meet your needs in such a way that you invite peace and fulfillment in, regardless of what you want in life.

When it comes to your feelings, lagom encourages you to cry as much as you need to and laugh as much as you need to. To listen to and embrace your emotional needs more than your wants. To find your perfect space of contentment between outbursts and internalization. And, more importantly, to proudly own that space without shame.

Because when you center yourself emotionally, you can enter various groups with a level of confidence that can withstand external forces pushing against you. You enter a shelter of contentment where you can exist silently and comfortably within a group without feeling the need to fill every lull with fluffy words.

EMOTIONAL CHECK

● Perhaps the ultimate lesson here is to learn how to listen more and speak less.

● There are so many opportunities and details you can miss when you dominate conversations and take up space. This doesn't mean deferring to others, but rather giving them their own space to shine as well.

● You can learn to respect others more when you pause to listen to them, and vice versa..

● Is stating the obvious in conversations really necessary or could that time be spent talking about more meaningful things that enrich and teach?

● Could the envy you sometimes feel for others stem from the fact that you see them operating closer to their ideal lagom state when you could be focusing on finding your own balance?

● It's possible to cease to operate from a mentality of scarcity and move to an emotional space where there is enough to go around.

● When it comes to emotions and feelings, accept and come to terms with your needs rather than be ashamed of them. That will drive you closer to emotional contentment.

FOOD

+

FESTIVITIES

"The stomach is filled earlier than the eye."

Swedish Proverb

We are creatures of comfort and one of our cozy dwelling places lies within the framework of tastes, fragrances, and the familiarity of foods we love to eat.

Many of our pleasant memories during the day are clustered around those moments when we pour our first cup of coffee or tea of the day, bite into a freshly baked *kanelbulle* (cinnamon bun) while inhaling its sweet scent, pause from work to sit and lunch with colleagues, or prepare meals accompanied by the warm chatter of loved ones gathered around the dining table.

A large portion of our lifestyles center on what we eat and how we eat it, and so it's no wonder that lagom as a code for living also manifests itself within this space.

Swedes are great lovers of food. Not in the sense of indulging in everything that crosses their plates, but rather eating well in a conscious way that adequately nourishes both body and soul.

When lagom shows up while we dine and wine with others, it takes the form of moderation, not restriction or limitation, as one would expect when it comes to food consumption. After all, Sweden also gave us the word *smörgåsbord,* which translates to a "sandwich table" but is used to mean a wide spread of choices and options, usually within the context of a buffet.

Lagom is used to qualify and quantify how we want our foods: "lagom hot," "lagom salted," "lagom size." It helps moderate portions as well as afford us the perfect taste with the right amount of seasoning.

❝ In Sweden, the idea of "fitting in" through lagom also shows in our food. By making cooking nonexclusive yet not too simple. By not using too many spices or too little. By not eating too much or too little. In essence, Swedish food epitomizes lagom.
Margareta Schildt Landgren, Swedish food writer
and author of over twenty cookbooks
❞

Beyond moderation, when it comes to daily nourishment, lagom also wears its coat of social consciousness, which ensures our individual actions are in the best interests of the greater good. This is where lagom suggests we eat sustainably, ethically, and locally. It wants us to not only take care of our stomachs, but also our food suppliers and the products and produce they provide us with.

That's why food campaigns encouraging people to, for example, eat less meat or avoid tiger prawns due to the unsustainable and eco-threatening practices surrounding them, are often prevalent in Swedish culture. Lagom pushes us to continually ask questions about what we're eating and the choices we make. It demands that we refrain from excess and take only enough to satisfy us, which is often much less than what we want, to avoid waste.

Lagom's temperance can even sometimes be seen in compliments given after a decadent meal. An excellent review from an older Swede after a fabulous dinner could be, "*Det var inget fel på det här*" (there was nothing wrong with this).

A SIMPLE START TO THE DAY

Many psychologists recommend starting your day with some form of meditation or alone time, disconnected from technology, to clear your thoughts before the rigors of the day rush in. You are encouraged to de-stress as much as you can before responsibilities and commitments begin to layer your mind with worry.

Lagom takes this concept of early morning de-stressing one step further. It's not just about closing your eyes for a few minutes to focus on your breathing, but also simplifying your morning routine and habits to relieve pressure before you leave the house, and that includes what you eat to start the day.

We can clearly see lagom in action when it comes to the typical Swedish breakfast. Unlike full English breakfasts, which are mini-feasts laden with fried eggs, crispy bacon, baked beans, thick sausages, and black pudding, breakfast in Sweden borders on minimalism.

I've often said that the quintessential breakfast in Sweden mimics the culture's deep-rooted practicality and the popular design concept of layering, where each item is a building block. This Scandinavian modular approach to design means each piece can stand on its own as well as fit into a larger framework. The building-block notion is one reason why the Swedish brand IKEA remains so popular around the world. It is also why the Danish brand LEGO continues to appeal to us all, regardless of age. It empowers us with very simple tools to build what we like to fit our individual tastes.

This principle of layering is also evident in the Swedish breakfast. Its two building blocks are slices of a carbohydrate, such as crisp bread, thin bread (*tunnbröd*), or soft multigrain bread, and dairy, such as a bowl of vanilla yogurt or *filmjölk* (*fil*), sour fermented milk.

From these two building blocks, you can begin to build the Swedish breakfast. Top the first element, bread, with slices of cheese, cold cuts, bell peppers, liver pâté, sweet dill pickles, or boiled eggs, to name just a few options. Whatever you can find in your fridge that can be sliced or spread is fair game. The second element, dairy, is topped with muesli, cereal, or fresh berries.

This breakfast concept requires less preparation in the morning and allows you to build it up or down as you wish, based on how many layers of toppings you want on your bread or in your bowl. Lagom manifests itself in this "less is more" paradigm when it comes to breakfast, focusing on essential nourishment that meets your needs while eliminating one layer of stress as you get ready for the day.

THE DAILY RITUAL OF FIKA

It's often joked about that the three essential words every new resident in Sweden initially learns are *hej* (hello), *tack* (thanks), and *fika*.

Before we learned how to invite lagom into our homes, we learned a much sweeter Swedish word called fika (pronounced fee-car). This social act is often translated as taking a break (*fikarast*) or pausing (*fikapaus*) several times during the day to socialize with friends, loved ones, and colleagues over cups of coffee and pastries like cinnamon rolls or cardamom buns. A similar observance would be indulging in an English afternoon tea, with its variety of scones and sandwiches, but the main difference lies in the frequency with which we fika. It is very common to take a break up to three times a day to fika.

According to the International Coffee Organization (ICO), Sweden is one of the top coffee-consuming countries in the world. So the act of fika is a time-honored ritual within Swedish society.

However, the true reason we take several of these moments during the day isn't to gorge on cinnamon buns, but rather to center and reconnect with ourselves. To give our minds a rest and balance our thoughts, work, and emotions by communing on a human level with our friends, colleagues, and family. It's a social opportunity within our very busy lives to step back and breathe while pleasing our sweet tooth.

Working too much is an antithesis of lagom, amongst other acts of excess, and eating lunch at your desk, in front of your laptop, is commonly frowned upon. Work-life balance is collectively pushed within the Swedish psyche through lagom. Partaking in fika is an act of recalibration, so you can carry on processing the day from a point of balance and harmony.

The tradition of fika is firmly rooted in lagom.

" Fika is a state of mind, an attitude, and an important part of Swedish culture. Fika cannot be experienced at your desk by yourself because it is a ritual. It refreshes the brain and strengthens relationships. And it makes good business sense: Firms have better teams and are more productive where fika is institutionalized.

John Duxbury, owner of SwedishFood.com

"

Speaking of coffee, *mellan bryggrost* (medium brew) is the most popular choice in Sweden. Because many people have a hard time deciding between light and strong blends, and with the guiding spirit of lagom sitting firmly on their shoulders, they collectively gravitate toward the middle. Not too strong, not too light, just right. And just right in this case means the medium option.

This same logic also applies to milk: *Mellanmjölk* (semi-skimmed milk) remains the most popular choice on supermarket shelves, which means, in addition to its nickname Landet Lagom (the Lagom Land), Sweden also cheekily goes by the moniker Land of Mellanmjölk.

EAT AS YOU WISH... WITHIN REASON

If the daily tradition of fika is any indication, Swedes eat a lot of sweets, but within reason.

"One should eat, otherwise one dies."
Swedish Proverb

Otherwise, eating cinnamon buns several times a day, every day, would quickly pile on the extra weight. According to the Swedish Institute, the average Swede consumes an equivalent of 316 cinnamon buns a year in pastries. Needless to say, Swedes love their buns. Yet the latest obesity update report from the Organisation for Economic Co-operation and Development (OECD) puts the United Kingdom's prevalence for adults at 24.7% versus Sweden at 11.8%.

In addition to moderation, lagom within the realm of gastronomy often aims for realism while battling superfluous consumption. It pushes us to live lives that we can logically maintain. When it comes to our meals, lagom wants us to have realistic diets we can comfortably support daily. Not dire restrictions that put undue pressure on us and pull us from our internal place of equilibrium. Lagom wants us to take care of our needs and cravings in a way that's not too much and not too little. It pushes us to reach for that chunk of chocolate, but prevents us from grabbing several pieces.

When it comes to sweets, the average Swedish family of four eats roughly 1.2 kilograms per week. Most of this consumption occurs on Saturdays, in a tradition known as *lördagsgodis* (Saturday sweets). This tradition dates to the 1940s, when Vipeholm Mental Hospital in Lund, Sweden, carried out experiments on patients by giving them large amounts of sweets to intentionally cause tooth decay. By 1957 the research had uncovered a direct relationship between sweets and tooth decay, and so the Swedish Medical Board advised Swedes to eat sweets just once a week. Decades later, this tradition of moderation still exists in many Swedish households, and children have been conditioned to accept this self-discipline. They instinctively look forward to sweets as something they occasionally indulge in and not something to be devoured every single day.

A RETURN TO SIMPLICITY

Nordic cuisine has been all the rage over the last decade, in what has been termed the "New Nordic Movement," which casts the spotlight on fresh regional ingredients from northern Europe, including the Swedish kitchen. A manifesto was even conceived in 2004 to guide this movement as it exploded around the world in the form of cafés, restaurants, and other gastronomical experiences promoting the simple wonders of Nordic cuisine. The threads running through this culinary resistance against the status quo of excess was a return to natural tastes, seasonality, well-being, sustainability, and high quality.

While stereotypes linked to New Nordic cuisine involve foraging for wild chanterelle mushrooms and picking cloudberries and lingonberries from Arctic boreal forests, for the everyday man, it not only means reconnecting with the source of our food but also eating closer to that source. It means deconstructing our complex meals so we can fully taste and appreciate each independent flavor.

Whenever a "less is more" approach to living is discussed, then it's time to cue in lagom.

THE NEW NORDIC KITCHEN MANIFESTO

- To express the purity, freshness, simplicity, and ethics we wish to associate with our region.

- To reflect the changes of the seasons in the meals we make.

- To base our cooking on ingredients and produce whose characteristics are particular to our climates, landscapes, and waters.

- To combine the demand for good taste with modern knowledge of health and well-being.

- To promote Nordic products and the variety of Nordic producers— and to spread the word about their underlying cultures.

- To promote animal welfare and a sound production process in our seas, on our farmland, and in the wild.

- To develop potentially new applications of traditional Nordic food products.

- To combine the best in Nordic cookery and culinary traditions with influences from abroad.

- To combine local self-sufficiency with regional sharing of high-quality products.

- To join forces with consumer representatives, cooking craftsmen, various industries, researchers, politicians, and authorities on this project for the benefit and advantage of the Nordic countries.

Source: The Nordic Council (www.norden.org)

Eating with these principles in mind certainly isn't new for Swedes, even though this foodie movement has now seeped across the globe. When summer and autumn roll around, many Swedes can be found picking mushrooms in forests across the country.

Lingonberry preserve is as essential to Swedish cuisine as ketchup is to the UK as a condiment. It is used to garnish everything from meatballs and pancakes to oatmeal and blood pudding, but never as just jam on bread. Many people still make their own preserves from kilograms of the sweet and sour berries they pick themselves from the forests when in season.

This free access to nature is facilitated by a government initiative, *Allemansrätten* (everyman's right), which grants us freedom to roam and freely enjoy the outdoors, including camping anywhere we wish, picking any edibles we want, and relaxing wherever we want, as long as no signs forbidding trespassing are posted.

This cultivates a mentality of sustainability. We eat from our backyards, we source local ingredients, and everyone has fair and equal access to food and resources through Allemansrätten.

For us to really taste the quality of a product, it needs to be stripped down and bared. Pure quality can be savored in the splendid combination of slowly cured salmon (*gravad lax*), yellow almond potatoes, and sweet tangy mustard, or the tasty marriage between wild game meatballs and the zesty sweetness of lingonberries.

Swedes also have their own soul food, from which they draw comfort. The Swedish equivalent of country-style cooking is called *husmanskost* (house owner's food). For centuries, Sweden was a working-class agricultural nation, where meals were primarily focused on starches you could pull from the fields, wildlife you could hunt in forests, seafood you could catch from the North and Baltic Seas, and endemic herbs that grew in subarctic forests.

Simple and inexpensive, husmanskost slowly made its way into taverns in the early 1900s, where it has stayed until present day.

Like warm blankets we've reached for since childhood, Swedes hold on to their traditional dishes amidst an ever-changing culinary landscape, and many of their high-quality products and produce, such as lingonberry, serve as durable, versatile, multipurpose food items which continually satisfy various food needs.

For example, you will readily find a crisp bread called *knäckebröd* in most Swedish homes. For over 500 years, crisp bread has been baked in Sweden. It is one of the most versatile food items in the Swedish pantry and can last for up to a year if properly stored. It can be eaten with sliced boiled eggs for breakfast, ham and cheese for lunch, or with plain butter as a side dish at dinner. This basic staple is not only practical and multidimensional, but it also epitomizes lagom when it comes to food.

Simplicity is in and complexity is out of the Swedish kitchen. Wherever there's a match where complication loses, lagom is right there, sitting on the sidelines, cheering on the side of ease.

ACCESSIBLE QUALITY FOR EVERYONE

Along with the New Nordic Movement has come the rise of fine dining and Michelin-starred establishments. They cater to the globally curious epicurean vying for a seat at tables minimally lined with handpicked berries and mushrooms, seasonal vegetables, ecological seafood, and game hunted by the chefs themselves.

While this might mean only those of us who can afford this luxury are invited, and it feels like an economic departure from Sweden's ideals of accessibility and equality for everyone, you might be surprised that, once again, lagom has raised its head within this space of high-end luxury.

The rise of exquisite dining experiences has also seen the rise of *bakfickor* (back pockets). These are affordable restaurants and bistros which are sisters to the Michelin-starred haunts, run by the same chefs. The concept behind these bakfickor is to provide value for money and make high-quality food accessible to you and me without special table reservations. This may mean the same quality of food but in different portions and at more affordable prices.

Lagom once again mutates and takes on the shape of social consciousness and fairness, aiming to make sure none of us feels left out of the team. Lack of access often breeds resentment between the haves and the have-nots, and in turn fuels discontent within our own lives.

A food culture built on openness and accessibility diminishes our inherent need to overconsume and to hoard away for ourselves, because like the average Swede, we know we can access what we need, when we need it.

This in itself feels like a luxury by virtue of geography. Yet it aims to keep lagom within the Swedish culinary lifestyle; a sense of "eating what we need when we need it" with no barriers to entry.

FEASTS AND THE ART OF REUSE

Before the Swedes gave us lagom, they also gave us smörgåsbord.

This Swedish word refers to a buffet-style spread of warm and cold dishes. We often use this word in everyday English to represent a large mix of variety, for example, a smörgåsbord of features or a smörgåsbord of activities. In the sixteenth century, a small buffet with schnapps and hors d'oeuvres was served as an appetizer before dinner within upper-class circles.

During the seventeenth century, these offerings expanded to include a wide array of foods, including salmon, cured meats, and sausages. And by the early twentieth century, the quintessential smörgåsbord had made its way into restaurants to be served to the masses, providing fair access to food experiences once reserved for the wealthy.

Even crayfish parties (*kräftskivor*), which are thrown all over the country during the months of August and early September to honor these crustaceans, were reserved for the upper gentry and aristocrats only in the sixteenth century. Over time, that wall of privilege has been brought down to provide access to this tradition across all classes of society.

Today, the Swedish smörgåsbord—often further shortened to *bord*—is the base feast for every major holiday we celebrate, starting with Easter (*Påsk*), to Midsummer (*Midsommar*), and ending with Christmas (*Jul*).

The main foods which make up the bord—meatballs, cured salmon, pickled herring, potatoes, and mini sausages called *prinskorv*—remain the same across all these different types of seasonal feasts, for the most part. These are the building blocks and it is through peripheral dishes like deviled eggs (Easter), strawberries (Midsummer), and cooked ham (Christmas) that foreigners know which seasonal smörgåsbord they are looking at. There's also the sweet root-beer-like soda (*Must*), which is renamed each season—*Påskmust* or *Julmust*.

This simple approach to reusing and layering has worked its way into how we celebrate and feast. We build and scale our smörgåsbord according to our individual tastes. Even the way and order in which we work our way through the smörgåsbord is a practice in lagom itself. Pacing is an essential art. It's often easy to spot the uninitiated at the table, for they have already filled up on the cold dishes before even anticipating the warm dishes or the sweets to follow.

Swedes even have a cake that works for several occasions and often appears in various forms. The princess cake (*prinsesstårta*) is a yellow sponge cake layered with jam, vanilla custard, and whipped cream, all sealed beneath a layer of colored marzipan and topped with a pink sugar rose. The cake was conceived by twentieth-century food author and governess Jenny Åkerström, who attended to Prince Carl Bernadotte's daughters, thus inspiring its name—princess cake.

While the classic version is green, today it appears in various colors to celebrate milestones—yellow for Easter, pink or blue for a new baby, and even as the "White Lady" with a white marzipan coating and chocolate mousse filling.

Once you start replacing unnecessary options and exorbitant alternatives with less choice, not only does it help reduce waste and unwarranted stress, but it also helps you focus on increasing the quality of what you truly need.

You wouldn't settle for low standards if whatever you chose was meant to continually meet and fully satisfy your needs over and over again.

FOOD FOR THOUGHT

▶ Reassess what you do around your breakfast table every morning and identify small ways in which you can de-stress before heading to work.

▶ Continually asking questions about what you eat and why you make the choices you make can help you eliminate what you truly don't need to consume.

▶ A lot can be said for taking multiple breaks during the day to indulge in the tradition of fika. Even a five-minute break will help to clear your head and reconnect with yourself.

▶ Should we consciously start making desk lunches a thing of the past? No matter how pressing a project might seem, you owe it to yourself to put your proper nourishment first.

▶ At your next meal, try skipping the condiments so the natural flavors and quality of whatever you're eating rise to the surface.

▶ Review the New Nordic Kitchen Manifesto and look for ways of applying it to your own life. It could mean visiting local farmers' markets, learning what is grown and raised in your own backyard, and finding out how you can support these local businesses.

▶ Maybe it's time to allow yourself to eat whatever you want within reason and in moderation. It's easier said than done, but lagom demands it in order to push our lives into harmony and give us more realistic eating habits that we can sustain.

▶ Having less choice allows us to focus on improving food quality.

HEALTH

+

WELL-BEING

"The deepest well can also be drained."
Swedish Proverb

It's often said that the best way to take care of your loved ones is to love and take care of yourself first. This means being in tune with your own body, addressing those needs first, and prioritizing your well-being.

Lagom operating within this space means harmony and balance. As that unspoken guide, lagom leads you to that perfect space in your life where you are naturally healthy—in mind, body, and spirit.

It wants you to get adequate rest for your mind, regular exercise for your body, and enough time alone to nourish your soul. More importantly, lagom wants you to do this in ways that are not too excessive and not too neglectful—but in the form of habits you can logically and realistically maintain.

Above all, lagom wants you to deeply assess and individually ask yourself the question: What does living well mean to me?

To live a life of harmony, you need to push yourself closer to the answer you come up with.

" Well-being begins with the simple question—what can I do to feel content and balanced? Asking this question shifts our whole perspective. We are empowering ourselves to explore what we really need and to evaluate for ourselves what makes sense.

Dr. Mary Jo Kreitzer, founder and director of the Center for Spirituality & Healing at the University of Minnesota

"

REDUCING EXTERNAL STRESS FACTORS

Often, the very best intentions we have for our lives are disrupted by external forces beyond our control. Taking enough time for rest and relaxation may be hampered by our working conditions and personal commitments.

Reducing these stress factors promotes our overall well-being and an improvement in well-being directly impacts overall quality of life. This is why the Swedish government has stepped in over the years to help reduce external stress factors around its citizens.

According to the United Nations (UN) 2030 Agenda for Sustainable Development, Sweden's third goal behind no poverty and zero hunger focuses on good health and well-being.

> " Good health is fundamental to enabling people to achieve their full potential and contribute to the development of society. Investments in health, for example through healthcare systems, are a reinvestment in the development of society as a whole.
> **Government Offices of Sweden**
> "

This means ensuring that everyone in Sweden has the opportunity to live their healthiest lives possible, and the government sees this as a fundamental right to well-being.

Sweden aims to do this by providing access to heavily subsidized medical and dental care (free for children and teenagers) and affordable, nutritious food, as well as pristine water, air, and natural resources in a clean environment that facilitates comfort and contentment.

In addition to this, Swedes get generous amounts of time off to spend in that never-ending quest to find a healthy work-life balance. A minimum of five weeks' vacation is standard for employees. Paid parental leave is 480 days (roughly one year and three months) per child. Now imagine having multiple children and multiplying that number, and you'll begin to understand just how much subsided time parents get off work.

There are at least eighteen public holidays as well as *klämdagar*, the days between a public holiday and a weekend, which some people can take as a holiday too. Many businesses often run reduced hours during klämdagar. You can also take compensated time off, a temporary parental benefit called VAB (*Vård av barn*), to care for a sick child.

While all this time off is certainly seen as a luxury by many, it is heavily subsidized by a tax system where everyone pays their fair share so everyone is afforded these basic rights.

According to the OECD Better Life Index, 81% of people living in Sweden are in good health, which is substantially more than the OECD average of 69%. The Swedish government gives them part of the solution and they come up with the rest to push themselves closer to their optimal well-being. Once outer forces such as worrying about access to healthcare or taking time off work are greatly reduced, they are granted the mental and emotional freedoms to focus on their individual well-being as part of the equation.

MASLOW'S HIERARCHY OF NEEDS

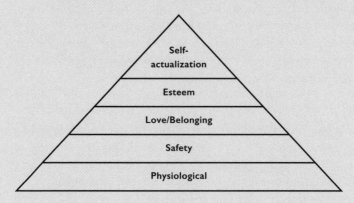

Conceptualized by American psychologist Abraham Harold Maslow, the theory known as Maslow's Hierarchy of Needs illustrates how innate human needs are activated.

Here is a summary:

Physiological Needs

Basic biological needs such as air, food, water, and constant temperature.

Safety Needs

Safety and security needs such as shelter and job security are activated once all physiological needs are met.

Needs of Love and Belonging

When safety and physiological needs are met, this triggers the need to give and receive love and affection to combat feelings of loneliness.

Needs for Esteem

As we satisfy needs moving up the pyramid, the need for self-esteem as well as recognition and respect from others is activated. Once satisfied, this builds a person's self-confidence and sense of worth.

Needs for Self-Actualization

Once all the other steps in life are fulfilled, this activates the person's intrinsic need to live out their authentic selves, share their talents with the world, and fully step into their personalities.

THE ART OF RELAXATION

If there's one thing Swedes have mastered, it's the art of taking care of one's self. After all, they did inadvertently inspire the Western-coined term "Swedish massage." This does not just mean physically staying in shape despite their daily consumption of cinnamon buns during fika breaks, but also taking care of the mind and spirit through relaxation.

When it comes to rest and rejuvenation, lagom is always questioning you and trying to get you back to the center. It aims to realign you with your own core equilibrium. Lagom tells you to occasionally stop to take inventory of your well-being. If something feels off-kilter, then work toward fixing it, whether that means actively working to reduce stress touchpoints, your blood pressure, or the number of commitments you take on.

Relaxation means cleansing your mind and detoxing your body. This could be a five-minute morning ritual or a solo retreat weekend every other month, but the goal of consciously taking yourself off-line is to slow down and listen to your mind and body, addressing whatever they require from you.

Because Swedes get as much rest as possible to subconsciously appease lagom as their guiding spirit, the region has produced many soothing relaxation traditions over the centuries. These range from bath houses, spas, sauna therapies, and herbal treatments to the famous Swedish massage.

Developed in the nineteenth century, the Swedish massage is often credited to gymnastics practitioner Per Henrik Ling, who introduced the concept to the West in the 1800s as the Swedish Movement Cure. This full-body massage uses various techniques such as long strokes, stretching, and kneading to improve blood circulation and relax the tissues and muscles, as well as rid the body of toxins.

When it comes to taking care of yourself, lagom wants you to be selfish about your well-being.

Meaning, since lagom prioritizes your needs over your wants, it wants you to make sure that your physical and emotional health needs are fully and sufficiently met first.

Often, what you feel you want may just be a semi-opaque cover over what you truly need. Your individual path to well-being is unique and requires self-awareness of where you are in your life and what you need at different stages.

By peering through the veil and addressing those core demands, you can begin to live a healthier, more energized and balanced life filled with contentment.

" The safety of our welfare system (the Swedish Model)
allows us to relax and focus more on ourselves,
our well-being and self-fulfillment (in line with
Maslow's Hierarchy of Needs).
Dr. Karin Weman,
Lecturer in Exercise Psychology at Halmstad University "

GUARDING PERSONAL SPACE

Considering that 97% of Sweden is uninhabited which works out at about twenty people per square kilometer, it's no wonder Swedes like to spread out. During the summer, many hide on various archipelago islands for weeks. On public transportation and in public spaces, people keep an adequate lagom space between them. This often means all available spots will be taken before someone will sit next to you. Foreigners should not take this personally; Swedes just like their space.

Lagom is very much at play here, taking on the form of appropriate social conduct and mindfulness, where you need to measure how much you inconvenience others, and they do so in return.

Similar to the silent code of Swedish restraint, Swedes selfishly guard their personal space, which is often perceived as individual bubbles of mental well-being. Anything along its periphery that tries to barge its way in or strain that circumference of personal comfort adds stress.

Lagom battles undue stress at all cost.

It wants you to be selfish about making sure your individual lagom ideals are met, including shifting and modifying your environment and the spaces that encircle you to make sure you feel comfortable, with no disrespect meant to the other party.

THE POWER OF NO

Swedes are direct when it comes to taking on extra responsibilities. They'll let you know right away if they can or cannot do something. There is no beating around the bush, or wavering or wallowing in feelings of guilt, especially at work.

> **"Better an honest 'no' than an insincere 'yes.'"**
> **Swedish Proverb**

A part of this lies in the fact that Swedish, as a language, is very direct and tends to get to the point rather quickly instead of wasting time with extraneous words. For example, "I am walking over there" in Swedish means *Jag går dit*, which translates to "I go there." Short and sweet.

This natural frankness of the language coupled with the underlying moderation of lagom means Swedes communicate in a brief, straightforward style that may come off as rude or standoffish to outsiders.

This also means they can be quite brutally honest when sharing their opinions on a topic or situation—how you look in an item of clothing, for example. Compliments aren't doled out easily because lagom coupled with its cousin, jante, wants actions to speak for themselves.

The pressures we exert on ourselves often come from overcommitment. We have a hard time saying no to friends, family, and colleagues. We often interpret our refusal to take on those tasks as personally rejecting them as opposed to just rejecting their inconvenient requests. They may also pull out guilt cards and file away our refusals as coming from a malicious place.

But to a Swede raised with the art of lagom, "no" often comes with zero personal strings attached. This helps manage expectations and frees us emotionally so we can continue to move along our individual lagom tracks.

ROUTINE EXERCISE + ACTIVE HABITS

If a Swede asks you to go jogging with them at a lagom pace, take a moment to step back and ask for clarification because as we now know, lagom is different for each of us.

A leisurely pace for you may mean breakneck speed for me.

While lagom, within the realm of exercise, might want to manifest itself as "just enough," maybe even bordering laziness by doing just what is adequate, the opposite is actually true. Consistency comes from habits and routines you can logically support, and lagom wants you to live a fully sustainable life.

This means regular exercise that you can maintain without dropping off the wagon, active habits that you seamlessly weave into your lifestyle so they don't feel like chores. For the average Swede, this could mean biking to work every day instead of hitting the gym after work.

Because of an intimate relationship with nature cultivated from youth (which we will explore more in a subsequent chapter), Swedes have fully embraced the concept of *friluftsliv* as part of their overall well-being. This principle directly translates to "open or free-air living." Coupled with Allemansrätten (every man's right), which grants free access to nature, they prefer to exercise outdoors amongst the elements.

This could mean cross-country skiing during winter instead of using the skiing machine in the gym, and biking everywhere instead of taking a spinning class. On vacation, Swedes naturally gravitate toward active vacations that ensure they spend quality time moving their bodies outdoors.

According to the Swedish Sports Confederation (*Riksidrottsförbundet*), 3.4 million residents between the ages of seven and seventy years are members of sports clubs, 45% exercise at least three times a week, and 2.4 million compete regularly.

" Many Swedes acknowledge the beneficial effects of exercise and physical activity. We have a long tradition of exercise and outdoor-living and we cherish closeness to nature, along with a "healthy mind–healthy body" belief.
Dr. Karin Weman, lecturer in Exercise
Psychology at Halmstad University "

These are impressive numbers considering the population size—roughly 10 million—and they speak of a society that runs on the tenets of lagom where regular exercise is seen as a lifestyle virtue, not a novelty, a bothersome chore, or a royal pain.

HEALTHY DISCUSSIONS

**"To write well and to speak well is
mere vanity if one does not live well."**
Bridget of Sweden (1303–1373)

Lagom's austere qualities can paint a picture of Swedes as a conservative and reserved bunch. But their beliefs and public actions are anything but old-fashioned and tame. The Swedish reserve comes from the fact that Swedes won't be overtly expressive without solid reason, but they are not demure to the point of nonexistence either.

Lagom encourages them to meet their basic human needs, which fosters contentment. This creates an openness and broadmindedness when it comes to talking about very natural topics, such as sex or even toilet habits, which other cultures may deem inappropriate.

There is a certain frankness when discussing sexuality and bodily functions, as well as a more comfortable approach to nudity than many other societies have. Subjects that are deemed natural and intrinsic are often fair game for open discussions, while those that are more superficial, such as your personal income, or socially uncomfortable, such as immigration and integration, are often avoided. This can be perceived negatively, because lagom's natural inclination is to avoid conflict and discomfort when it comes to extremely important dialogs that need to be had within a society.

Lagom releases that cultural strain that says you can't talk about topics that are essential to your humanness. It stipulates that there is no shame to hide, no apologies to be given, and no self-consciousness to feel when it comes to living your optimal life.

SELF-CARE

💜 Constant connectivity impedes on your ability to live a more balanced life, so maybe it's time to schedule a digital detox?

💜 Learn to say no more often. We often get pulled into unnecessary tasks that waste our valuable time. By constantly taking a step back to assess a request before responding with a resounding "yes," you can begin to weed out irrelevant work.

💜 Ask yourself this question: What does living well mean to you? Does it involve regular exercise? Adequate alone time? Meditation? Write down your own list.

💜 Create measurable goals that you can logically stick to. Why sign up for a marathon if you haven't been running regularly, when you can start with a 1.5-mile jog around your neighborhood?

💜 Take small steps in building daily habits. Routines come from consistency, not duration. The key to unlocking balance is to maintain consistency in your life.

💜 Learn to listen to your body and mind through adequate rest.

💜 Be compassionate with yourself. It's okay to fail but it's important to get back up and start over again when you're ready. And only you know when you're ready.

💜 The more we openly talk about natural topics such as sex, the less sneaking around the subject we do as a society.

BEAUTY

+

FASHION

"This is no bad weather, there are only bad clothes."

Swedish Proverb

Beauty is certainly in the eye of the beholder, and when it comes to how lagom manifests itself when we dress our bodies and present our faces to the world, it waves the "less is more" flag.

It chooses a subtler, more natural aesthetic than an attention-grabbing persona. Because lagom fights extremes, it encourages us to choose logically and practically. It wants us to be informed about the products and clothes we invest in on a regular basis.

We all have different tastes in clothing or makeup. Some of us are more daring than others, prefer heavier makeup than others, would choose a well-tailored suit over casual wear, or heels over flats. Lagom doesn't try to change our individuality, and it doesn't push us into whatever realms we consider "mediocre."

Rather, it wants us to find our own set points that we can logically maintain. It wants us to choose versatile, durable products that can sufficiently meet our beauty and fashion needs without overextending us financially.

Swedish women love their makeup. That doesn't mean it is applied in heavy-handed strokes. On the contrary, it's an understated affair, used to subtly enhance features rather than transform one into a totally different person. Beauty is low-key, and with some underpinnings of jante in the mix, we as individuals are not to feel like we're better than anyone else.

While outsiders may see this as chipping away at one's self-esteem by not fully stepping into and owning one's beauty, on the contrary, lagom wants the world to see and appreciate our natural beauty without hiding it under layers of makeup.

> " The Swedish approach to beauty is very minimalist,
> and everything needs to function effectively in our
> busy everyday lives. Taking care of the body from inside
> and out is just as important as taking care of the
> face with good beauty products. Anything you
> can easily reach for in your handbag for a quick
> touch-up during the day is a winner.
> **Linn Blomberg, makeup artist
> and Nordic beauty consultant** "

A Korean beauty brand called LAGOM, with its tagline "Not too little, not too much," has even seized on this concept of "less is more" and is building its business on a framework of casual skincare routines, packaged very simply.

There's also a UK fashion brand called Lagom that aims to interpret lagom in the form of effortless style. A lot of money goes into looking casually thrown together. That pair of blue jeans and beige cashmere sweater that look well-worn may actually have cost a pretty penny and may have just been purchased the day before. Overtly standing out from the crowd, where all eyes are drawn to us, can in turn make us uncomfortable. The goal is not to be unkempt either, but rather casual chic.

Lagom tries to narrow down our choices to simplify our lives and create some balance. Too many options can have a crippling effect.

In an article in UK-based *Red Magazine* imploring us to detox our wardrobes, writer Amy Davidson urges us to declutter by pulling out clothes we haven't worn in over a year because chances are, if we haven't donned them in twelve months, we probably won't wear them during the next twelve months.

PREPAREDNESS AND PRACTICALITY

As the old Nordic adage goes, there is no bad weather, only bad clothes.

This is about preparation and the need for practicality over primp. By virtue of their climate and northern location, Swedes have been raised on cold, harsh winters that plunge the country into long spells of darkness. For at least five months out of the year, Swedes are in several layers of clothing that can be peeled off and slipped back on as they move from warm cozy interiors to frigid outdoor temperatures. This also means at least five months where practical shoes such as low-heeled boots are required, lest they slip and slide on icy surfaces.

The ever-changing, challenging Swedish weather has in many ways informed the culture's fashion sense. It requires preparation and this often comes in the form of layered looks that you can mix and match.

So go for sturdy clothes that meet your needs against the elements first. After all, winter gear can be expensive and constantly replacing clothes can easily dent the wallet.

" In Sweden, winters are long and summers short. Swedes dress for comfort and warmth during the winter and celebrate the sun by wearing as little as possible during summer.
**Dr. Philip Warkander, Assistant Professor
in Fashion Studies at Lund University**
"

That said, because quality is essential to an item we often must reuse several times, the Swedish fashion sense is also one of practical quality that many are willing to pay for. They tend to opt for simple yet high-quality and well-made fabrics over quantity.

Lagom says your clothes have to attend to your basic needs for a very long time. So, invest in the best quality you can afford.

VERSATILITY OVER VERSACE

" For such a small country, our fashion industry is surprisingly
strong and well developed with brands that have gained
international reputation, such as H&M, Acne Studios, and Our Legacy.
**Dr. Philip Warkander, Assistant Professor
in Fashion Studies at Lund University** "

While you'll spot your fair share of high-end designer brands in Sweden,
fashion here is simple, relaxed, and very casual. Stockholm Fashion Week,
held every winter, brings out the understated Swedish style in full display
with clean lines and layered looks.

Even within formal business settings, jeans with a long-sleeved
shirt and maybe a sweater is perfectly acceptable as professional office
wear. Unless, of course, you're meeting with foreign clients who are used
to suits and ties or are attending board meetings with key stakeholders
or investors.

Even so, Swedes gravitate toward versatile outfits that can be mixed, matched, and reused in several ways. That long-sleeved black shirt that can be transformed from workwear to after-work lounge garb just by adding a necklace, or that sweater dress that can be dressed up or down by adding a belt.

This doesn't mean Swedes are always clad in monochromatic tones, however. They are open-minded when it comes to fashion and are often seen as early adopters as well. From plaid-wearing, fully bearded looks to clean-cut urbanites with slicked-back hair and from those wearing bold floral prints to colorful patterns, individual style is essential.

But ease of access makes it easier to dress similarly as well. To the majority, individual style can be challenging since jante, on lagom's back, doesn't want you to stick out. People blend in because they don't want to stand out in a way that draws uncomfortable attention.

So, you'll find hordes of "individuals" with similar looks. With fairness and accessibility always in the Swedish consciousness, this is one of the reasons why Swedish fashion brand Hennes & Mauritz (H&M) remains quite popular around the world. It aims to give us a glimpse into the simple, versatile, mix-and-match world of affordable Swedish fashion.

When it comes to lagom within the sphere of your attire, logically pick the item that has multiple uses over the one-use novelty item that will no doubt sit in the back of your wardrobes for months.

RECYCLED FASHION

" In Sweden, the question of sustainability in fashion has
become increasingly dominant. There is a consciousness that
is impacting how we talk about fashion, and how we see ourselves
as not only consumers but also as citizens and humans.
Dr. Philip Warkander, Assistant Professor
in Fashion Studies at Lund University "

Because Swedes require durability to continually meet their needs, they invest in high-quality fabrics and materials when producing clothes. Plus, in a culture built on reuse, recycling, and sustainability, it's no wonder there is a slew of vintage and secondhand shops dotting the country. And even more interesting is that they are regularly frequented by many sections of society.

One of Stockholm's edgy districts, a former seventeenth-century slum neighborhood called Södermalm, arguably has more vintage stores per block than any other area in town. Even the glitzy, upscale district of Östermalm has its fair share of antique shops.

A lifestyle operating on lagom will always choose quality over quantity, even if that quality is found in a secondhand store.

BEST FOOT FORWARD

● Sounds like it's time to simplify some of your beauty routines. Maybe institute "no makeup" days to give your skin a break.

● Proper hydration is one of the best skincare regimens you could ever give yourself so make sure you drink adequate amounts of water daily.

● Take time to clean out your closet. Do you really need five similar-looking black lace dresses or white shirts? If you haven't worn an item in at least twelve months, maybe it's time to sell or donate it.

● Indecision often stems from the fact that we have too many choices. Maybe reducing your choices when it comes to clothing and beauty products can assuage some of that indecision.

● A fun exercise next time you go shopping is to look at an item on a rack and visualize how many ways it can be dressed up or down, paired with accessories. If you can think of five different looks, you just might want to pull it off the rack and add it to your collection.

● Would you ever consider visiting a vintage or secondhand store? Many of the items for resale in there are actually made from durable, high-quality material, which is why they have lasted for decades.

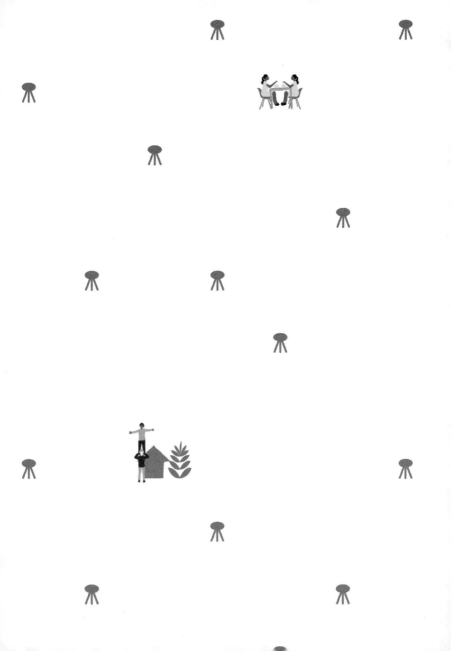

DECOR

+

DESIGN

**"Away is good,
but home is best."**
Swedish Proverb

Our inherent need to explore the world and travel its farthest reaches is tempered by our need for security, safety, and a nest of familiarity we can call our own. We seek that comfort within our dwellings, where we can retreat from the elements and shelter before we set out again.

A new generation of millennials includes digital nomads who move from place to place, exploring and creating temporary homes around the world. But no matter how temporary or permanent the nests we build are, the very basic human fact remains that we all need one. And if we can afford it, we deck out those nests to suit our tastes.

We create homes that reflect who we are as people.

If there's one sure thing Sweden has given the world beyond musical talents, noir films, and sturdy station wagons, it is its minimalist Nordic approach to design and decoration: durable, high-quality items designed to weather the changing seasons with aplomb while looking effortlessly chic where they stand.

> "
> "Swedish grace" was an early British description of quintessential Swedish design about a century ago. More elegant than our Nordic neighbors, yet not as monotonous as the European design of that era. In a way, it still stands over time.
> **Claesson Koivisto Rune, Swedish architectural partnership**
> "

CREATING HARMONY AT HOME

Because lagom ultimately wants you to find your symmetry and to live well, it tries to remove the stress factors all around you to create calm and peace.

When it comes to decorating your home, lagom pushes you toward personal effects, emotional items, and aesthetic elements that make you happy or bring some sort of joy. It could be that wooden elephant you brought home as a cheap souvenir from Thailand or that vintage armchair you saved for months to buy.

It wants you to invite harmony into your home by avoiding clutter and balancing practicality with memorabilia near and dear to your heart. Even better if a single item can fulfill both roles of functionality and sentimental value. Everything outside those two main categories—practical and emotional—can be considered unnecessary excess.

> **"** "There's nothing wrong with mixing old and new, with combining different furniture styles, colors, and patterns. Things that you like will automatically fuse to form a relaxing entity."
> **Josef Frank, nineteenth-century**
> **Swedish-Austrian architect and designer**
>   **"**

Lagom wants your belongings to either have a logical purpose or bring you joy. The ultimate goal is to create a warm place that makes you happy and instantly calms you down the minute you walk through your doors. Achieve this with the scents that evoke that special feeling of belonging, the plants that bring a bit of nature into your dwelling spaces, a palette of your favorite colors, and the photos and decorative ornaments that adorn your walls and shelves.

This concept of creating harmony extends beyond Swedish lifestyle. The Taoist concept of feng shui, with deep roots in China, aims to harmonize you with your environment. It believes that there are invisible energy forces that bind us all together, and these forces need the freedom to move and flow without interruption. Feng shui principles can be applied to the way you build and design your home to ensure this seamless flow.

While Swedish design has no roots in spiritualism, it seeks the same goal of harmony by creating spaces that evoke feelings of contextual perfection and allow you to feel at peace in your very own lagom nest of contentment.

"

HARMONY AROUND THE NEIGHBORHOOD

Backstory: a closer look at classic Swedish cottages

Classic *stugor* (cottages) add bursts of rich, red color
as you move across Sweden's lush countryside. This deep,
coppery shade—Falu red—is named after the town of Falun
in Dalarna, where it originated. Between the sixteenth and
nineteenth centuries, this paint was the cheapest available.
So many cottages had that same rich, cozy hue.

If you had a bit more funds, you could paint your cottage
yellow or white. But that was about the extent of showiness
allowed. I wonder how people gave each other directions
before the invention of road signs.

"Go down the road until you see Nilsson's red cottage,
then turn left and keep straight until Arvid's red cottage
comes into view. Take a quick right at Sven's red
cottage before you finally arrive at Olof's red cottage."

Lola A. Åkerström, *Due North: A Collection of Travel Observations*

"

ELEGANCE IN SIMPLICITY

When it comes to inviting lagom into your home, simplicity is best.

Instead of seeing your home as a finished painting, lagom wants you to simplify it back to blank canvases so you can create spaces of living art where elements can be mixed and matched, moved around and pieced together like building blocks—the underlying ethos behind IKEA's DIY appeal where each element can function individually and collectively.

Lagom wants you to opt for a "less is more" approach when it comes to your interior decor. It wants you to see the chicness in clean lines, the tastefulness in sparseness, and the sophistication in reserve, and to build a solid base of neutral colors upon which you can expand. That foundation of neutrality helps put your personal pieces and keepsakes in the spotlight within your home.

As discussed so far, when it comes to deciphering lagom, it says that your needs supercede your wants, and so you must focus on quality, durability, and practically first to comfortably address your needs.

- For a piece of furniture or item to be practical, it has to be simple and very easy to use.

- To meet your needs consistently, it needs to be made of high–quality, durable materials that will last a long time.

- Because it is designed to last a long time, it is something you will look upon time and time again, so it has to be aesthetically pleasing.

These three tenets are what lie behind quintessential Swedish design: function, quality, and looks.

> " Good design is an effort to achieve a certain timelessness in our work by avoiding current trends. Good, quality materials and skilled craftsmanship are part of this equation.
>
> **Claesson Koivisto Rune, Swedish architectural partnership** "

Looks can also be deceiving.

That angular, futuristic-looking chair that screams typical modern Scandinavian aesthetics has been ergonomically designed to fit and mold to your spine for maximum comfort. There is a deep consciousness and thoughtfulness when it comes to design, all wrapped up with the elegance of simplicity.

Remember, functionality rules lagom, no matter how aesthetically unusual a piece may be.

Thoughtful design

Swedish design continues to push the boundaries of innovation and sustainability. Furniture designer Monica Förster created a line of office chairs, Lei for furniture brand Officeline, which are ergonomically tailored for female bodies for maximum support while working.

> "
> "I wanted Lei's form to be dictated by its functions, measurements, and technical solutions, all of which are grounded in extensive ergonomic research focusing on what women need from an office chair, and how they sit differently than men."
>
> **Monica Förster, Swedish designer** "

FOCUS ON LIGHT, SPACE, AND PATTERNS

Swedes are obsessed with light.

Any form of light is greatly revered. This basic instinct to always seek out light was born from centuries of having to survive through long, dark winters. Those first glimmers of sunlight which signify the approach of spring are often soaked up with fervor.

From cozy candlelight on tables to warm lamplight at doorsteps to guide the path in the dark, luminance in all its modes is essential to Swedish culture.

In Sweden you'll find airy abodes with space cleared to allow light to flow from lamps. These could be anything from standing and table lamps, to candleholders and paper lanterns to chandeliers and spotlights.

Illuminating the Swedish home is a serious endeavor which rivals that of picking out your sofa.

Light brightens the home and metaphorically brightens the soul. It chases away dark despair and offers glimmers of hope within the daily toil. Lagom wants our homes—our happy places—to be as incandescent as we can afford to make them.

We've also learned how much Swedes value their individual space, so even the tiniest of apartments will often look breezier than normal because they have been consciously designed to maximize the space within them.

For all our talk of neutrality and simplicity, Swedish homes are not devoid of vivid colors or patterns. Different textures and shapes are often sprinkled around the home in the form of the fabrics used in pillows, casual throws, bedspreads, and napkins.

From nautically inspired stripes of white and navy blue to the instantly recognizable eighteenth-century Swedish folk pattern of vivid floral patterns called *kurbits*, the textiles chosen often meet both the requirements of functionality and sentimental value. Towels, pillows, and napkins are incorporated into everyday use, yet their designs gravitate toward color and geometry, giving a glimpse of personality.

The fabrics we line our nests with play a significant role in creating our harmonious spaces of warmth where we feel physically at peace.

> "
> Strong colors and patterns can remove the feeling of confinement. Even the smallest compartment can be exciting with a striking wallpaper.
> **Josef Frank, nineteenth-century**
> **Swedish-Austrian architect and designer**
> "

LIVING SUSTAINABLY AT HOME

While we will delve deeper into the overall Swedish psyche when it comes to sustainability later in the book, it is important to explore it within the realms of your home and choices.

Because in addition to creating your ideal dwelling, lagom wants you to be able to logically maintain it in an affordable and sustainable fashion. It wants you to find that healthy balance between your individual needs and the needs of the environment you find yourself in.

This means cultivating habits that will not only sustain you within the home but are also socially responsible and environmentally conscious. It means using what you need in just the right amount so there is enough to go around that adequately meet the needs of others around you.

VIRTUE IN MINIMALISM

Undue pressure comes from trying to maintain a lifestyle you can't sustain. By constantly asking yourself questions about the choices you make, you realign yourself and find your perfect space.

Why maintain a house if a large apartment will suit your needs just fine and eliminate the stress of additional maintenance?

When it comes to creating your ideal home, lagom invites you to make small changes that enhance the quality of your life.

The virtue of minimalism is that it psychologically frees us from unnecessary tasks and responsibilities that weigh us down. In addition to this freedom, it also lets us see our own tastes and preferences more clearly against a clutter-free backdrop.

When your natural inclinations and tastes are exposed, you can begin to build your own spaces of recognition, security, and harmony.

" Minimalism is not about deprivation. It's about finding more value in the stuff you own. Minimalists do this by removing the superfluous, keeping only the possessions that serve a purpose or bring joy. Everything else goes by the wayside.
Joshua Fields Millburn, one half of The Minimalists
"

HOME IMPROVEMENT

🪑 Lagom isn't urging you to dramatically redesign your home. After all, that would be unrealistic and expensive. What it wants you to do is honestly question why you own a piece of furniture or item that is taking up space.

🪑 Start decluttering by making two lists—practical or emotional. Anything that falls outside of these categories is fair game for removal.

🪑 Let there be light! Try to brighten up your space using natural or artificial light sources. Studies have shown that we are drawn to light because it subconsciously lifts our spirits.

🪑 It might be time to do some rearranging of furniture, especially if you've been looking at the same layout for years. We naturally like symmetry and are pulled toward visual balance.

🪑 If you don't have ultimate control over the decor where you live, create your own happy, clutter-free corners, designed in your favorite colors.

🪑 Bring fresh plants and flowers into your home to clean the air and promote overall well-being.

🪑 Have you considered upcycling? This means repurposing an item and giving it another function instead of throwing it away.

SOCIAL LIFE

+

PLAY

"Seriousness and pleasure should thrive together."

Swedish Proverb

We are social creatures who seek solace and comfort from one another.

We long for acceptance, we crave belonging, and we subconsciously need the proximity of others to keep loneliness at bay. We often thrive better emotionally within cultures where there are social frameworks that treat everyone as family and focus more on the "It takes a village" mentality when it comes to interacting with each other.

However, in cultures that focus more on individuality and self-sufficiency, clouds of isolation can form at the peripheries. We feel excluded and secluded more often, and there's a magnified sense of being an outsider, regardless of intent. Making friends seems more challenging, building an active social life feels a lot more like a chore than it needs to be, and we may plunge into mental spaces of desolation more often than we'd like to.

Such is the case within the Swedish society, running on the guiding principle of lagom that stipulates we take care of our individual needs first and make sure we don't aggravate our neighbors in the process.

This unintentionally creates a society of interiority where people are open-minded enough to allow their neighbors to do whatever they want yet keep very close bubbles around their lives that exclude external stress factors, discomfort, and the unfamiliar.

So I've often said that Sweden is the most open society run by the most private people.

When it comes to how we move and interact within society, as well as entertain ourselves, lagom shifts into its role of appropriateness and fairness. And whenever lagom rears its head within group settings and pulls us out of our focus on individuality, its jealous cousin, jante, is often close behind, bringing some negativity with it.

This is also why, putting aside individual personalities, socializing with a Swede abroad and one back home in Sweden can be very different experiences. Because lagom can be slinked in and out of like lingerie, Swedes abroad are often quick to shed lagom and the appropriateness it requires in group settings, due to its perceived unattractive traits. Many Swedes abroad brag about their country, but once back on its shores, they firmly criticize it.

So what can lagom truly teach about when to socialize and play with others?

LOYALTY AND SOLIDARITY

Regardless of whether we are natural introverts or extroverts, we want a culture that allows us to carve out whatever social life we want for ourselves with minimal effort.

"If you play the game, you accept the rules."
Swedish Proverb

As we've already explored, lagom's culturally accepted roots are firmly entrenched in team dynamics, something that supposedly goes back to the Vikings. The word itself is a shortening of the phrase *laget om* (around the team), so naturally, lagom is more transparent in social settings and is easier to measure within this context.

Because of its "different strokes for different folks" approach, lagom frequently shifts our focus from self to group, to ensure we aren't encroaching on other people's rights. It seeks deep loyalty from others who share the same philosophical approach to living and aims to build solidarity around our metaphorical team within society.

This is often why new residents in Sweden find it hard to make long-lasting friendships from the get-go. It seems Swedes have very small personal circles of friends, many of which have known each other since childhood. To join that team as it stands requires absolute trust and loyalty, and there's often a tempered discontent voiced when non-team-like behavior is observed.

If our eyes are the windows into our souls, then the natural inclination of Swedes toward prolonged eye contact over body language can be a personal assessment. While sustained gazes might seem unnerving to other cultures, a Swede is subconsciously thinking: Can I trust you enough to fully invite you into my world?

Once that outer shell has been cracked, you may be on your way to netting yourself a Swedish friend for life because lagom is tightly tethered to trust, fairness, and loyalty.

Like a rugby scrum forming on a pitch with forwards tightly locked and ready, lagom, as scrum half, trusts we are 100% ready in our positions to receive the ball, that ball signifying what we hold most dear to our hearts.

After all, lagom aims to create contextual perfection and balance around us. It wants us all to be reliable team players that can be trusted to do what we say we will do and mean it. There's a sense of security—*trygghet*—that comes with this trust and loyalty.

And this is also why Swedes thrive within organized activities, sports, and other types of clubs that meet regularly.

"
The Social Framework

Swedes socialize through what I call "frame activities." You first sign up with an organization, a sport group, or any type of organized activity. The idea is to do something practical first, then after some months (or years), you may be invited for a one-on-one non-framed activity like dinner or coffee.

Another form of framework are quizzes and games, which Swedes will gladly use during parties or other social gatherings in order to get people to feel comfortable enough to interact with others they do not know.

These frame activities remove the Scandinavian awkwardness of speaking with someone they do not know, providing a secure framework for interaction so they are not left not knowing what to say!

Julien S. Bourrelle, author of *The Social Guidebook to Sweden* "

Even outside of clubs and groups, social frameworks have been put in place to create these organized, rather unspontaneous environments for socializing, from *hostlov* and *sportlov,* which are one-week vacation breaks during the autumn and winter, respectively, when everyone is collectively given permission to go hang out with their families on active vacations, to *fredagsmys* (cozy Fridays), when families stay home and curl up in front of the television with snacks and entertainment.

Lagom, beyond the individual, always craves context and order.

QUIET CONFIDENCE VERSUS SHOWING OFF

When it comes to lagom, actions speak so much louder than words.

"Self-praise smells bad."

Swedish Proverb

While many cultures are more open when it comes to bragging or gallant displays of victory, lagom wants you to temper your emotions with a cool restraint, because you shouldn't make others feel too bad when you celebrate your triumphs. Everyone is entitled to some level of happiness, even when they are on the losing side of the game you just played. If in doubt, watch a Swedish TV show where a participant has just won a million *kronor.* Their subdued physical reaction to the news will most likely be different from yours.

Children are taught at an early age, within various scenarios, not to compete, that they shouldn't feel they have to be better than anyone else. The most important thing is to participate.

This burden of fairness that comes with the ethos means that bragging and bravado are often frowned upon, yet winners feel like they can't fully revel in their joy without judgment. This can feel at odds with lagom's core tenets, which want you to take care of your needs first and

find your personal equilibrium while somehow expertly balancing all this against the needs of the group.

So how are you to navigate these murky waters of celebrating the self against the strong tides of the group?

This is often when opponents of lagom raise their hands to ask the following questions.

Can't we fully enjoy our achievements and publicly celebrate them? Why should we take on the unnecessary burdens of other people's feelings toward us? After all, haven't we rightfully earned our victories through hard work?

Wait…are we actually looking at lagom at play here or have we confused it with its cousin, jante?

Remember, whenever lagom manifests itself within groups, jante is right behind, bringing with it jealousy and judgment, because my lagom isn't your lagom.

If we pull off the jante mask and reassess the situation, we would see that lagom truly wants to push us to a space where we can balance our feelings in a sustainable way, one that doesn't pull us toward both extremes so frequently that it derails and weakens us, sentimentally, which can also be perceived as emotional imbalance. There's a certain innate self-confidence that comes from letting our work do the talking.

Constant boasting can often erode expectations and unwittingly put pressure on us to over-perform and overachieve. If we can't meet what we initially promised, this quickly begins to erode trust and reliability. A mentality of lagom deeply fears this erosion of trust.

Even going on a date means putting on our investigative fedora hats and fishing out information with tons of follow-up questions because Swedes don't casually throw out accomplishments—or any personal information for that matter.

> " The concept of lagom has created a culture of fairness and trust. It holds back conspicuous consumption and selfishness, and makes sure that the whole team—might it be a school, a company or indeed, the whole country—gets their fair share.
>
> **Dr. Kjell A. Nordström,**
>
> **Swedish speaker, author, entrepreneur, and economist** "

Watching how Swedish athletes react on global championship stages is a quick lesson in lagom. They've been culturally conditioned to temper their emotions and instead, let their prowess do the talking. Responses are measured with the right amount of perspective, without being lackadaisical about accomplishments either because, after all, they've worked really hard.

Celebrating feats of success is done in moderation, though this is slowly changing due to the diversity of culture and emotion that athletes who are second-generation immigrants bring to the table.

When expectations are exceeded, athletes' responses to their amazing performances when interviewed could be:

"I guess I was okay, it was the team that won."

"I do my job for the team."

"As long as we win, it doesn't matter who scores."

Because Swedes generally don't use a lot of body language to communicate or display too much emotion, they must often rely on words to explain how they are feeling. Unfortunately, the Swedish language is a very direct one that gets to the point rather quickly. So there are very few elaborate adjectives or flowery words to convey emotion.

A fantastic soccer game could be communicated as *Det var otroligt!* (It was unbelievable!). Adding the word *helt* (completely) to the mix is about the extent of heightened expression the language reaches: *Det var helt otroligt!* (It was completely unbelievable!)

Lagom can be misinterpreted as timidity, but that couldn't be further from the truth. Lagom implies moderation on one's own terms. It's a way of setting expectations, so when we do meet or exceed them, we are perceived as operating with high standards.

Plus, once we realize we're the only ones showing off time and time again, we'll begin to understand unspoken codes of conduct.

SELF-SUFFICIENCY
WITHIN SOCIAL SETTINGS

Going back to humility, it's best to disassociate this word from lagom.

"Pay back with the same coin. (Get even.)"
Swedish Proverb

Yes, Swedes can be shy and bashful around strangers and in situations that feel uncomfortable and unfamiliar. After all, this is a natural response to the unknown as we try to decipher and understand each other. But humility denotes a certain servility, subservience, and submissiveness that borders on timidity. These words are often in direct contrast to a culture that thrives on direct communication with a direct language.

Because everyone is supposed to be treated equally and fairly in a seemingly egalitarian society, lagom as a fierce idealist doesn't want us to be subservient to each other. It wants us to walk side by side on equal footing, though not necessarily with arms linked.

While lagom is considerate to its neighbors, it isn't intrinsically service-minded based on the fairness and equality factor. It wants us to be self-sufficient islands of independence, indebted to no one. It wants us to only take what we absolutely need from society while leaving enough to go around. It wants us to try to solve problems to the best of our abilities first before seeking outside help.

There's even a Swedish proverb that states that you are your own best helper.

This game of self-sufficiency is played out in various social contexts but especially when it comes to shopping or dining out. Attendants rarely hover over you while shopping, wait staff rarely visit your table until you make eye contact and wave them over. For people from cultures that are a lot more service-minded, these attitudes might come off as flippant or nonchalant.

Restaurant bills are almost always split and very quickly too, before one of the guests causes an awkward scene by trying to cover the entire bill. For someone going on a date, expecting to be wined and dined, this cultural norm can come as a surprise at the end of the night. Swedes are conditioned to split their bills to always repay favors and not be duty-bound to anyone, especially financially.

Remember, lagom strives for balance, and any gestures that haven't been adequately reciprocated are seen as throwing off that equilibrium and tipping the scale heavily to one side.

This subconscious self-sufficiency also manifests itself within romantic relationships, where it is common for unmarried couples to pair up for years and even have several children together, yet live financially independent lives. Many reject the notion of marriage, which is often perceived as an eternal dependence on another individual.

How can you find your own level of lagom if you're constantly dependent upon or emotionally obligated to someone else?

THE ART OF PATIENCE

While our current world of instant gratification and overstimulation fueled by social media is continually weakening our ability to exercise patience, let's cue in lagom and see what it tries to teach when it comes to the art of restraint.

"One can never wait too long for something good."
Swedish Proverb

When you practice lagom in your life, this does not automatically mean that you are immune to restlessness and discontent. But it is worth noting that there is an arena where stress, unnecessary conflict, confrontation, and impatience is kept at bay.

To avoid potentially charged social situations, Swedes have been conditioned to queue. While this might evoke images of lemmings in a line, this is a mental state of preservation that is automatically invoked when we walk into a place of business.

If you enter any store, pharmacy, deli, government office, or bank in Sweden, chances are there's a numbered queuing system in place. Ticket machines dispense printed numbers, which are displayed or called when it's your turn to be served.

While queuing and ticketing systems are by no means special to Sweden, the sheer frequency with which you find these machines—often ironically hard to find once you're in place—helps to cultivate patience and peaceful frames of mind. Because you are already going into a situation with expectations of waiting, you mentally prepare yourself, plan accordingly and, above all, de-stress, knowing you will have to be patient. Lagom naturally fights all forms of stress like the plague and it proactively puts measures in place to avoid confrontation and ensure conformity within the group.

RESPECTING TIME

Lagom not only demands that we respect ourselves, but others as well, by living according to the golden rule: Treat others as you would like to be treated. Give them the space they need and don't waste their precious time or resources either. By cloaking itself with the cape of appropriate social conduct, lagom aims to respect everyone around it and not hinder others. We should be able to comfortably share space with others without devaluing them and their time.

This virtue is evident when it comes to punctuality.

Swedes are well-known to be a very punctual bunch at home, work, and play. Kids arrive at day care on time, adults arrive at business meetings on time, and on social occasions, friends start drinking their cocktails on time. Public transportation runs on time. Agendas are followed on time, as schedules can go into disarray otherwise.

While many cultures have a more laissez-faire and optimistic approach to time management, a lifestyle running on the thread of lagom says that my actions, when it comes to time, must not encroach on the comfort of others. If two people have decided on a time, then they need to honor their word.

If you can't be trusted to show up when you say you will without a solid explanation for your tardiness, how can you be trusted when brought into tightly knit inner circles of friends?

After all, lagom draws strength from trust to build loyalty.

TIME OUT

- When it comes to social life, lagom's strength lies in teamwork. It wants us all to be reliable team players. When was the last time you gave your all to a team?

- Keeping bragging to a minimum can infuse the element of surprise into your relationships. Why not pleasantly surprise that new acquaintance by not showing all your cards at once? Admiration is often built up this way—the seductive art of measured revelation.

- Maybe it's time to join a club to keep your hobbies alive. Start swaying to salsa music, strumming the guitar, playing rugby, or painting again. In this way you could create a solid social life filled with passionate people.

- Swedes naturally keep eye contact when talking, and you could also hone our yown skills of looking others straight in the eye. Sustained eye contact evokes a sense of self-confidence.

- Do what you say and mean what you do. This can be accomplished by not overpromising and creating logical parameters around what you can and can't do. You can let your actions speak for themselves.

- If you've had a problem with people not trusting you, it's never too late to start picking up the pieces. Not by telling them what you think they want to hear, but rather, by being direct. An honest "Sorry, I can't" is always better than a failed promise.

- If you're a time optimist, tardiness disrespects people's time.

WORK

+

BUSINESS

**"A business is good when
both parties make a good bargain."**
Swedish Proverb

The world of business is cutthroat. We fiercely compete to stay afloat. We accumulate outstanding personal achievements to get ahead. We chase career dreams with a passionate unyielding focus. We often define success based on winning. From scoring coveted clients and lucrative projects to marketing ourselves as the perfect solution to fixing problems for others.

Sometimes we win at the expense of others in the name of "good" business. We gain as much profit as possible while spending as little as we can on resources. After all, business thrives at the intersection of competition and individualism, and how well we sell ourselves and our work. So it would seem lagom would already be choked out of this space before it even tried to raise its head.

Yet it barges its way through, waving the flag of fairness and logic.

If you take a closer look at the Swedish proverb stating that good business is achieved when both parties make a mutually beneficial bargain, you can begin to see how lagom manifests itself in your work environments and the businesses you run or take part in.

It shows up in the way you interact with your colleagues and in the differing approaches you take toward working on a common goal. When it comes to earning your keep, lagom wants you to approach work with a strong ethic wrapped in fairness, loyalty, and trust. The very same virtues it craves in your social life when you play with others, it requires when you work with others professionally.

When it comes to the workplace, where the greater collective good must be achieved for the business itself to be good, lagom consciously switches you into team mode. This means stitching your business cultures with threads of rationality, wrapping cloaks of loyalty on its shoulders, and pulling belts of trust around it.

It chooses logic over emotion. Practicality over vision. Action over promise. Lagom wants your actions and the words you speak to be binding long before you physically sign any contracts.

> " The Swedish approach to work and business is one of loyalty and trust. Swedes have always identified themselves with their work. While millennials may not be as loyal as older workers to an employer, a level of loyalty still remains.
> **Tünde Schütt, professional head hunter
> and job coach for Swedish-based firm, Develop Me** "

PLANNING AND PREPARATION

Swedes have been conditioned to always be prepared. Centuries of living with unpredictable weather conditions, amongst other circumstances, has built a mindset to be properly prepared to face any challenges the day might unexpectedly throw.

Readiness requires planning. It's no surprise that this mentality of proper planning would make its way into everyday work lives where unpreparedness can destroy a project or even bring down an entire company.

Many foreigners working or doing business in Sweden often lament the amount of time Swedes put into up-front planning and preparation. Agendas are triple-checked and several meetings are called to plan every single item on said agendas. Plans can take months to put in place before moving to the next step of implementing each item on those plans.

For a culture that prides itself on efficiency, these inherent acts of zealous planning can be seen as counterintuitive and as wasting time and resources.

However, because lagom craves balance by trimming excess around its edges, it requires adequate planning. "Adequate" is measured by whatever it takes to prune irrelevance, regardless of how long it takes.

To be efficient means to perform and function in the most optimal manner possible with the least wastage of time, resources, and energy. This very definition of efficiency mirrors the core of lagom.

So lagom says it is perfectly okay to spend as much time as needed to prepare yourself and strongly develop your plans because that's the only way to guarantee efficiency.

THE IMPORTANCE OF CONSENSUS

Lagom at work completely shifts into team mode. It moves responsibility and accountability from the individual to the team. And there's really no way to fully break out of this mentality when working with Swedes.

If you're coming from a culture where one person always calls the shots, you may have mixed feelings when met with the lagom approach to business. In advocating for equality and fairness on all levels, decisions are often made by group consensus.

Everyone has to agree on everything on the agenda. Otherwise, another meeting will be organized to find out why everyone isn't agreeing on everything on the agenda.

A typical Monday morning could start with an overall status meeting and continue on throughout the day with several follow-up meetings to address individual items on the agenda that were already discussed in the overall status meeting held in the morning.

Meetings are called to debate, discuss, and decide on what may be perceived as mundane subjects to an outsider. If consensus can't be reached, a fika break with coffee is in order, and then it's time to reconvene at the table once more.

This might frustrate you if you're looking to take quick, decisive action. Or you could embrace it with open arms because, finally, your thoughts and opinions will be actively considered in decision-making.

If you look closely, you'll realize there are a few things at play here beyond the annoyance that gathering in multiple meetings may cause.

First, lagom thrives on fairness and equality.

It naturally encourages and invites participation so all our voices and individual opinions are heard.

Second, lagom is always looking for the optimal balance, so it seeks collaboration and finds ideal solutions to problems through consensus. Lagom naturally questions all actions to find the best answers. It wants us to be open-minded about this intrinsic quest for contextual perfection by being logical and objective, rather than emotional.

Lastly, the need for fairness and equality breeds a flat business structure as opposed to the hierarchical pyramid structures we commonly find in companies around the world. This management style invites more casual, transparent access to upper management. So ideas can feed up to managers in a relaxed, campfire-like setting where everyone can speak their minds.

It's very common to casually call your company's CEO by his or her first name. After all, the lagom mindset says we're all fundamentally equal and should be treated that way, regardless of our social titles or cultural standing.

In terms of gender balance in the workplace, Sweden ranked fourth globally on the World Economic Forum's Global Gender Gap Index in 2016. It achieved this by closing 81% of gender-based inequality and continually fostering representation and diversity.

So when it comes to making decisions, it is a very inclusive process that ensures we're all working together to meet a common goal. It fosters compromise by removing emotion and inviting logic. It promotes teamwork, which further builds loyalty.

"Sweden's very relaxed structure in terms of corporate hierarchy means managers are not demigods. Managers cannot give out orders. He or she has to convince their employees through diplomacy about the direction they want to take or the goal they want to reach.
**Tünde Schütt, professional head hunter
and job coach for Swedish-based firm, Develop Me**
"

THE ART OF NEGOTIATION AND CONCISENESS

Swedes often make great negotiators. Not the ruthless kind because, after all, good business must adequately satisfy both sides without making enemies in the process. This penchant for diplomacy comes from lagom and its need to continually ask questions.

Sentimentality is left outside the door of the boardroom and pragmatism is given the steering wheel. Items are discussed in detail, proposals are questioned in depth for viability, and negotiations often leave no stones unturned.

While this might seem exhausting if you find yourself sitting across from lagom, this natural need ensures that whatever business actions taken are the very best decisions for the group to ensure balance and harmony.

This also means a certain conciseness when it comes to communication. As we've already discussed, this comes from having a very direct language as well as looking at chitchat and extra words as unnecessary and inefficient. So Swedes tend to get right down to the business at hand. Interactions are often direct and to the point. Emails reflect this concise style as well. Business is conducted on facts, not intuition. Negotiation is done in a very methodical way.

Getting to the crux of what needs to be addressed quickly helps to remove distractions that can steer away from solving problems, so harmony can be achieved once more.

While the overall responsibility for a project shifts toward the team as a whole, lagom holds you personally accountable for what you say you will do, in an effort to maintain trust and dependability.

If you fail, the team might take one for you, but they will no longer trust you and this would be reflected in those typically Swedish prolonged stares of assessment every time your eyes meet. Conflict and competition

Lagom metaphorically dies at the intersection of conflict and stress. It shrivels up at any potential sign of confrontation and hates to be pulled off its equilibrium. This clearly manifests itself in the work envrionment and places of business.

"One who proves too much proves nothing."
Swedish Proverb

After all, if you achieve consensus, you reduce the risk of conflict afterward, right?

Since everyone already agreed to the same course of action, no one can technically be angry with you, right?

This is also why Swedes are masters of saying "no," although this is gradually changing due to external pressure from a society that expects us to be superhuman, because "no" can be perceived as incompetence.

Rejecting additional work is important because accepting it may strain your ability to deliver on your promises, thus resulting in professional conflict or strife of some sort. Credibility is fiercely guarded by setting realistic expectations and keeping promises. And this is done by taking on tasks you know you can fully complete so you don't erode the trust your colleagues have in you.

It's not uncommon to firmly refuse work from your boss without feeling guilty or thinking it will automatically affect your relationship with them. Lagom is direct, and those who operate and live according to this principle have a deep understanding about this.

Creating a relaxed environment at work by removing stress is important, from taking a more casual approach to business dress codes to making enough time for fika breaks to recharge before jumping back into the race.

Swedes who are brought up to instinctively navigate their way through team dynamics know the exact measurement of lagom that needs to be applied in different situations.

When it comes to individual competition, Cousin Jante forces itself in on the coattails of lagom and tries to put everyone in their place. It says we shouldn't feel and act like we're better than others, that boasting is a sign of poor self-esteem and a lack of confidence in letting one's work speak for itself.

While this might be in direct odds with the corporate world, where you need to compete to survive in the marketplace, lagom tries to focus on quality, and it wants that quality do the selling for us. This doesn't always work, especially when actively marketing oneself and capabilities is often seen as a necessary investment to succeed in business. In essence, selling the work before it has actually been done.

But if you push Cousin Jante back out the door and refocus on lagom, you can begin to understand why individual competition is not only frowned upon, but perceived as unsustainable, and frankly, a waste of energy. I liken it to trying to keep pace with a well-seasoned marathoner when you're running your first race.

Lagom cannot be measured equally.

My lagom is not your lagom. Instead of competing, it wants us to find our own equilibriums, activate our individual competencies, and identify our core strengths. Constantly focusing on individual gains means you lose sight of the team's business goal.

The optimal solution comes when everyone confidently steps into their roles based on their own strengths and internal lagom markers, and not through personal competition.

Yes, competition can be healthy and can give you that extra push. But that shove needs to consciously steer you toward finding personal harmony and balance. That competitive push shouldn't derail you from your path in life.

GIVING AND RECEIVING FEEDBACK

We often hear the phrase "No news is good news," meaning if we don't receive feedback, chances are all is well and we don't need to worry. Well, this is easier said than done.

"No letters are good letters."
Swedish Proverb

We put our best foot forward and naturally worry when we don't receive verbal confirmation. After all, how else can we assess if what we're doing is in line with what the team needs? And isn't it nice to get that occasional pat on the back to boost morale and fan our flames of loyalty?

When it comes to the typical Swedish workplace running on lagom, personal feedback can be hard to come by, despite Swedes being very direct in the way they communicate.

Compliments aren't easily strewn around because the lagom mentality always focuses on actions first. It takes its cue from the things we do and pairs them with what we say to see if there are clear disconnects. Plus, not giving constant appraisals is another way of avoiding confrontation that may bring discomfort and stress.

There are obvious advantages and disadvantages to this moderate approach to giving feedback.

The main advantage is that lagom runs on trust and so you're operating within a team that clearly trusts your capability and competence by not constantly micromanaging you.

To achieve lagom, strive for a balance between celebrating your successes and continuing to do your job with a strong work ethic. If you constantly tout your accomplishments, it can create an exhausting environment and relationship with others. As in the story of the boy who cried wolf, they may fail to properly recognize your good news the moment you need their recognition the most.

The clear disadvantage is the underappreciation you might feel if you are resigned to a corner without enough personal assessments from your peers and managers. As creatures who thrive on acknowledgment, we all need recognition once in a while, to affirm that we are not only doing things correctly but doing them exceptionally well too.

SETTING PERSONAL BOUNDARIES

"Empty barrels rattle the most."
Swedish Proverb

That intense, sustained look. Hanging onto your every word, head slightly cocked to the side with deep interest while you speak…No, your Swedish colleague or boss is not desperately in love with you.

On the contrary, lagom breeds a nation of excellent listeners who give you space to finish your train of thought without rudely interrupting. After all, that would be an inconvenience to the other party because lagom aims for a harmonious exchange free from interference.

In addition to giving respect, prolonged eye contact is a sort of quiet assessment of trust and the opportunity to gauge how much to open up to you and share in return. It doesn't mean the Swede has feelings for you. The uninitiated among us may often misinterpret such focused attention as personal interest.

But rather, it's about waiting your turn to speak without interrupting and talking over each other. It really is all about respect.

Also, don't be fooled by those casual business settings with an air of informality and accessibility. Swedes keep very firm lines between their work lives and their private lives. Personal information isn't readily shared even if one tries to pry it out.

Colleagues do enjoy after-work drinks together and participate in various social clubs and activities together. They may even hang out socially so frequently that one might think that the next logical step would be an invitation to dinner. But playing within those social frameworks doesn't mean you're moving closer to being invited across that professional line into private homes and personal lives.

FINDING WORK-LIFE BALANCE

Sweden has some of the most generous working hours in the world.

With five weeks of vacation instituted by law, 480 days of paid parental leave, over a dozen holidays and other paid time off to take care of sick loved ones, it's no wonder Swedes are often out of the office the minute the clock strikes five, if not earlier.

Several companies have even been experimenting with six-hour days, to see if working shorter hours would improve efficiency while guaranteeing that healthy work-life balance Swedes passionately protect.

After all, lagom aims to work effectively by crafting a life you can comfortably sustain. It wants you to question why you are working overtime and to see if you can better allocate your time in order to rebalance your life.

When it comes to balancing the needs of your personal life with your career, lagom takes on the shape of moderation and sustainability. It wants to ensure that whatever decisions you make don't negatively impact your well-being.

This invites a certain flexibility into the culture where, for example, parents can leave work earlier to go pick up kids from kindergarten, duck out of the office for appointments, or work a reduced schedule between 50% and 75% if they want after they return to work from parental leave.

Unlike some other cultures, where strong emphasis is placed on working as hard as you can so you can accumulate as much wealth and success as you want, Swedes operate from a different angle.

Swedes work to live, not live to work.

Meaning, they work to earn enough to fully support their own individual levels of lagom in their lives. The presence of lagom as one's lifestyle principle means one doesn't feel the need to accumulate excess for the sake of perceived success. That is often why even the wealthiest of Swedes may have sparsely decorated homes filled with high-quality items.

I often recommend that visitors to Sweden get their shopping done before 6 p.m. because many businesses close by then. Sometimes earlier during the weekends, which often feels counterintuitive because most people are free then to catch up on their shopping. This work ethic, enforced by many trade unions, ensures that retail workers' rights are sufficiently protected so they can maintain balance in their own lives too. This in turn improves the overall quality of life across society.

DOING SOCIALLY RESPONSIBLE BUSINESS

Taking care of each other, as well as our environment, extends into the realms of the workplace and the way we conduct business. This virtue of social responsibility manifests itself in the way Swedes run their companies.

Because lagom fundamentally runs on fairness, equity, and sustainability, Swedish businesses are leading the way in terms of corporate social responsibility (CSR) worldwide. Global issues such as our impact on climate change, gender equality, environmental protection, human rights, and the fight against corruption are just a few causes a business operating on lagom wants to address. According to the Swedish Standards Institute, the country has some of the highest numbers of environmentally certified businesses per capita in the world.

So it's not uncommon to find CSR tightly woven into a company's strategy and its day-to-day operations. Lagom stipulates that our drive for profitability should not impede on the rights of others or negatively impact our society and environment.

While a subdued approach to competition, conflict resolution, and overall work structure might seem to mean that doing business with lagom lacks the lucrative opportunities expected in more capitalist models, we might want to reassess this notion.

In 2016, *Forbes* evaluated 139 countries for their business savvy based on eleven factors, which included innovation, taxes, technology, and bureaucracy, among other indicators. After this assessment, *Forbes* gave Sweden the top spot for doing business, ranking it number one globally. In comparison, the United States, known for its economic prowess and strong business culture, placed twenty-third, while the United Kingdom took fifth place. There's a lot to be said for inviting this ethos into our business lives.

MEETING MINUTES

- Learn to be more measured when it comes to decision-making and take an extra step back to reassess situations from one more angle before rushing into conclusive commitments.

- If you're in a position of power, creating a relaxing environment around you and your employees, as opposed to a tense one that only feeds your ego as a boss, can breed the loyalty you crave.

- Your credibility hinges on doing what you say you will do. So learn to say no, be honest about your abilities, set expectations, delegate often, and finish fewer tasks, but do them exceptionally well.

- If every single accomplishment is shared the minute it is achieved, the more important news will not make much impact on friends and colleagues.

- Do you really need to work overtime? If not, then ask yourself why do you do it anyway.

- While consensus has its time and place, getting a second or even third opinion on what you're working on may give you some much-needed objectivity on something you're passionate about.

- If you fancy yourself an excellent negotiator, take a step back to reassess what negotiation means to you. Are you always seeking to outsmart and outplay others by constantly leaving them with less? Or are you negotiating from a place of empathy for both sides?

- Be ready to ask questions and avoid taking things at face value.

MONEY

+

FINANCE

"Better a bird in hand than ten in the forest."

Swedish Proverb

If money is the root of all evil, then the lagom mindset—running on equality and fairness—has a very complicated and rather obsessive relationship with finances.

In a world where the gap between rich and poor is continually widening, it is no surprise that we all crave financial security. Since it costs money to meet our basic human needs, we often fear we may not have enough to address these physiological elements.

We worry about adequate shelter, food, water, and healthcare. We worry about the expenses tied to these core needs, from grocery bills to keep our stomachs filled, utility bills to keep our homes running, and medical expenses to make sure we stay healthy.

Many of us often worry from paycheck to paycheck because our responsibilities and commitments pile on faster than we can economically support them.

And for those of us who can comfortably meet our basic needs, we crave more money for the extra security and perceived peace of mind surplus brings. We want more money to be able to chase our desires, dreams, and wants without restriction. We seek not only financial independence but economic stability.

When it comes to money matters, lagom takes on the more logical and common-sense approach to managing the purse strings.

It wants us to balance our books by giving as much as we take. This naturally steers us away from debt. It espouses a more meticulous approach to handling money where we must sufficiently question why we make certain purchases. It tries to file the things we spend our hard-earned money on under two categories: functional value and sentimental value. Anything that falls outside these two lists can be considered excess or useless. And we already know that lagom naturally fights against superfluity with all its might.

So when it comes to money and finance, there are several ways lagom manifests itself. One involves alleviating financial stress by preparing for rainy days through taxation. Another means simplifying our spending and minimizing our financial lives to the point of perceived frugality. And a third manifestation wants us to adequately plan out where our expenses go every month through common-sense budgeting.

TAXATION AS STRESS RELIEVER

It's safe to say that money is a major source of stress in our lives. It's also safe to say that being a tax collector is one of the most despised and least trusted professions, dating back thousands of years across different civilizations and well into biblical times. After all, no one wants to part with cash they've struggled and toiled to amass over the years.

Yet there's a certain comfortable relationship with the Swedish Tax Agency among Swedes.

While citizens of many countries loathe paying taxes and would absolutely skim by on paying as little as possible while taking the maximum amount of deductions they can, Swedes have cottoned onto the fact that paying adequate tax can actually be a good thing, whether they personally like it or not.

> " The Swedish word for tax—*skatt*—has another meaning:
> treasure. There can't be many languages in which the
> word for tax has such positive connotations.
>
> **David Wiles, content director at Spoon Publishing in Malmö, Sweden**
> "

If we take a closer look at the word for tax in Swedish—skatt—it means treasure.

Taxes can be seen as a way of saving for rainy days throughout one's lifetime because the system is trusted and works well when needed. It ensures paid leave after having or adopting children, covers unemployment benefits after losing a job, subsidizes education and healthcare, helps us to pay rent if needed, and guarantees social security after becoming a pensioner, to name a few benefits.

All these personal situations can financially ruin an individual and quickly push them below the poverty line, yet Sweden as a whole strives for equality and ensures everyone pays their fair share so they can all live lives of suitable quality. This safety net greatly eases financial stress, and lagom will happily invest in any system or structure that reduces uncertainty and insecurity in our lives.

To create that sense of external stability and economic peace around us, lagom in an ideal world doesn't want us to stress too much about money. It wants us to work enough to sufficiently meet our day-to-day needs, knowing that we're contributing to that collective net of financial calm through paying our taxes.

Now, Sweden is known to have a high tax system. Oftentimes, other countries think this is reflected in their income tax, which isn't the case. The average personal income tax in Sweden ranges between 30% to 33%, while corporate tax is around 22%.

The real tax burden comes through indirect tariffs such as value added tax (VAT), which can add up to 25% to the cost of the goods and services. This is why spending is often kept to essentials that meet functionality requirements or items that deeply tug on the heart strings.

Regardless, paying taxes as a necessary evil is often addressed from a practical point of view. If taxation provides universal protection around us, we might as well embrace it, says lagom.

FRUGALITY AND BUDGETING

ᴵᴵ Swedes are very much into savings. We got used to this over time through government-backed fund savings in the 1980s. Saving monthly is now a very natural thing to do. From saving to first support one's own lifestyle and children to saving for retirement."

Ingela Gabrielsson, private economist and spokesperson for Nordea Bank Sweden ,,

After spending some time in Sweden or around Swedes, many foreigners may begin to detect a certain frugality and, sometimes, borderline obsession with prices.

This frugality is often at odds with a mindset that demands you meet your needs with the best quality you can afford so that it can sustain you for a long time. This means being conscious about the things you spend your money on and making sure they bring the right type of value into your life to keep it balanced.

Swedes like well-crafted things and this is reflected in the quality of the items they choose to surround themselves with. They also want to invest in those things only once. This means veering toward durable items made with high-quality materials, designed for long shelf lives.

This indirectly feeds into Sweden being an expensive country to shop in. In addition to all the value-added taxes, superior materials and organic ingredients that go into goods drive costs up.

Another element of Swedish prudence comes with the "waste not, want not" mindset of lagom. This can even be seen in a post war–era classic comic strip called *Spara och slösa* (save and waste), which taught children the value of saving and showed them the dangers of wasting.

By simplifying their day-to-day sustenance, they not only reduce waste, but also the pressure on their wallets. They find ways to upcycle the things they own by repurposing them and giving them another function instead of replacing them with new items.

Swedes dole out cash where and when it makes the most sense and look for free activities and good deals wherever possible, from free concerts and complimentary family activities held in various parks, libraries, and museums to remarkable steals while perusing second-hand flea markets, book sales, and other money-saving opportunities.

**"A piece of bread in the pocket is better
than a feather in the hat."**
Swedish Proverb

When it comes to creating budgets to help keep you on financial track, lagom's propensity for asking questions comes into play. It demands to know where each penny goes every day, every week, and every month.

Lagom says to use only what you need, and it tries hard to curb impulse-spending, which falls under acts of extravagance. It helps to track spending and find compromises in an effort to push you toward contentment in your financial life.

Even if you have very little compared to the massive wealth others may have, lagom wants you to focus internally first instead of measuring yourself against others.

As the Swedish proverb goes, it is better to have a piece of bread in your pocket than a feather in your hat.

This means it is always better to modestly meet your needs well within your means than to put on a grand display of a lifestyle you can't fully sustain financially.

> " On balance when it comes to investing, most Swedes land somewhere in the middle of risk and non-risk. Half of Swedes have a plan with their savings and the other half "just save."
> **Ingela Gabrielsson, private economist and**
> **spokesperson for Nordea Bank Sweden**
> "

Why invite unnecessary pressure into your life by living so far above your means that you are constantly unhappy, unsure, and insecure?

TACKLING DEBT

As discussed previously, living with the ethos of lagom means our lives exist alongside imaginary scales that always need to be balanced. Anything that tips that equilibrium strongly to one side or the other is seen as a burden. Lagom tries to recalibrate itself by getting rid of the overload.

Despite its focus on building harmonious communities around us, where we take care of each other, it also promotes self-sufficiency. This personal autonomy moves us away from individual indebtedness to one another. Debt weighs both parties down, thus causing stress. This pressure disrupts balance.

Lagom withers away with embarrassment under debt. Former Swedish Prime Minister Göran Persson was often quoted as saying, "The one who is in debt is not free." This by no means suggests that Swedes don't carry their fair share of financial debt. They do, especially when it comes to investing in their homes. However, debt is not a natural part of the culture, which strives for monetary independence.

While this sounds in direct conflict with Sweden being known as a social-welfare state that is economically dependent on the government, lagom's intrinsic mindset of paying with equal coin is why Sweden has some of the lowest national debt levels in the EU. In 2016 *Forbes* also ranked Sweden fourth in the world based on monetary freedom, and the Swedish government has been balancing its budget for over a decade.

If anything, lagom wants us to collect money directly from the communal pot we all chip into with our taxes and not necessarily directly from others, which is seen as being a burden on them.

WEALTH AND FAME

If you asked the average Swede to name one Swedish billionaire, they might immediately think of Ingvar Kamprad, founder of the globally recognized furniture brand IKEA.

Beyond Kamprad, they might scratch their heads trying to readily come up with other names. But according to *Forbes*, Sweden has more than twenty-five billionaires, with the richest man in the country being Stefan Persson, who owns an enviable chunk of shares in fashion brand H&M. The fact that these people quietly exist within Swedish society while amassing incredible amounts of wealth shows the temperance and discretion that comes with lagom.

Wealth isn't flaunted in the same way as we might see in the United Kingdom or the United States. But make no mistake, Swedes are certainly accruing riches at record-breaking speed. Start-ups based on innovation and technology are creating the next generation of entrepreneurial millionaires.

That quiet, unassuming stranger sitting right next to you on the subway train may very well be running the hottest start-up company in the market and raking in millions every year.

Wealth isn't worn on their sleeves. Yes, they might appraise the quality of the clothes they wear, the cars they drive, and the parts of town they live in as indicators of affluence. But estimating just how wealthy a Swede is remains quite the daunting task. This is mostly because Cousin Jante brings with it a whole lot of discomfort and subconscious shame when they brandish their successes.

Lagom tries to reconcile personal wealth and finances with the inherent need to overconsume and show off by adding that layer of moderation within spending habits.

MONEY MATTERS

🐷 When it comes to your finances, lagom doesn't want you to penny pinch. It just wants you to have a better grip on how much you spend so you can indulge occasionally to balance your life.

🐷 It's time to start putting away some money for a rainy day. While most of us don't have the benefit of a mature welfare system acting as a safety net, maybe you can start putting a little bit away into a savings account to relieve some financial stress.

🐷 Buy less, but invest in quality. Lagom says it's better to save up and buy one solid durable item than a dozen cheap ones.

🐷 There are many tangible changes you can start to make in terms of curbing your expenses, from bringing a packed lunch from home rather than eating out to limiting grocery shopping to once a week.

🐷 If you've never created a budget, now is as good a time as any to start recording your expenses. You don't have to start with elaborate spreadsheets; try a simple bullet-point list.

🐷 If you already work with a budget, maybe it's time to revisit it and see which expenses can be trimmed off, while bringing in more meaningful experiences that add value to your life.

🐷 It's time to get serious about tackling whatever debts are weighing you down. Talk to an advisor who can help you whittle down your financial burdens.

🐷 Living above your means is exhausting. Aren't you tired yet?

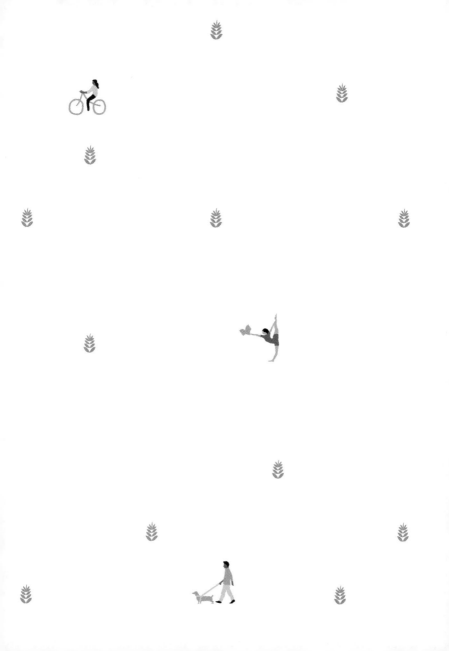

NATURE

+

SUSTAINABILITY

"He who saves, has."

Swedish Proverb

If there is one area where lagom truly shines, it is in our relationship with nature and the outdoors. It governs the way we think about our environment and wants us to see and process the world around us through a lens of sustainability.

Even Cousin Jante concedes defeat and bows out whenever Mother Earth and her natural resources are in the spotlight, because lagom's greatness virtue—mindfulness—is brought to the surface.

The Swedish lifestyle is intricately linked with nature. It is a very close relationship, filled with a respect which has been meticulously cultivated and promoted since childhood. There is an innate comfort that comes with spending time outdoors, communing with the elements regardless of temperature, and, above all, protecting it with a fierceness that may seem in direct contrast with lagom's self-control.

This comes from the fact that lagom naturally wants to make sure everyone has fair access to the same resources. When we take, we need to return whatever we've taken for someone else to appreciate too. Everyone must have an equal stake in both enjoying and replenishing the ecosystem we share.

In addition, the access we have to nature is perceived as a loan which must be paid with equal coin to achieve balance. Lagom consciously governs how many resources we consume and creates a mindfulness around that, which in turn breeds sustainable attitudes. What we borrow needs to be carefully tended to so we can return it in as near perfect a condition as when we first laid hands on it.

This careful maintenance and continuous tending is what sustainability, at its core, is all about.

FOR THE LOVE OF NATURE

" Through my years of research, I define "Nordic well-being"
as resting on the interface between everyday life and nature;
advanced simplicity in the design of what we surround
ourselves with; and accessibility to nature.

Julie Lindahl, intercultural expert and author of *On My Swedish*
Island: Discovering the Secrets of Scandinavian Well-Being "

Despite the calmness that comes with lagom's moderation, Swedes are uncharacteristically aggressive and proactive when it comes to conserving natural resources.

To fully understand how this loving protectionism has become deeply entrenched in the Swedish psyche, we need to step back in time to see how Swedes have interacted with their environment.

When it comes to spending time outdoors, come rain or shine, this collective mindset has been fostered by government policies.

Between late February and early March, Swedes take a winter vacation break from school in a cultural tradition known as sportlov. This vacation is meant to encourage us to spend time with our families in nature while participating in physical outdoor activities.

In 1925 a youth organization decided to arrange field trips to the mountains for interested grammar-school children. It wasn't until the 1940s that the government seized upon the opportunity to introduce a heating conservation initiative. Originally called kokslov (Swedish for the fuel "coke"), a mandatory school break was instituted in order to ration coal and coke which were the primary fuels for heating buildings after the Second World War. This not only meant a reduction in fuel consumption nationally but also gave students an opportunity to participate in organized field trips. By the 1960s the idea had expanded to save heating in offices too and had morphed into its new version, sportlov.

Now, pairing this with Allemansrätten (every man's right), which grants free public access to recreationally enjoy nature, the stage was set for cultivating an organic love of the outdoors from a young age.

Allemansrätten allows us to camp outdoors, cross-country ski and trek everywhere, unless signs prohibiting trespassing are in place. This right also includes picking wild berries and foraging for mushrooms to our heart's content. Allemansrätten encourages us to explore our backyards.

It doesn't hurt that over 80% of Sweden's residents live within three miles of a green park or nature reserve. And according to the

Outdoor Association (Friluftsfrämjandet), 97% of Swedes are in favor of protecting this access to nature as a basic right.

Mentioning the word "Skogsmulle" to any Swede is enough to conjure up childhood memories of the iconic outdoor wilderness character who taught them all about exploring and enjoying nature. Over 200 Swedish day-cares follow the Outdoor Association's recreational program called I ur och skur which means "come rain or shine."

From a very young age, children have been conditioned to spend time outdoors and in nature, and have been taught not to fear it. They no longer see time spent outdoors as compulsory exercise; it is now a basic necessity.

At day-cares and kindergartens, children are bundled up and left to play outdoors for hours under piles of snow. Even babies under six months are put outside for a few minutes to breathe fresh winter air.

While this cultural phenomenon may seem focused on physical exercise, the real underlying benefit is its creation of environmentally conscious citizens.

Free public access to nature means we all play an instrumental role in making sure that access remains free by respecting the land we tread on. Taking care of the environment becomes second nature because we spend a lot of time outside. In the same way that we regularly clean the homes we live in, our need to clean and protect the outdoors is strong.

This puts Sweden in a very sweet spot when it comes to selling the benefits of sustainability, eco-friendly initiatives and protecting the environment to its citizens. For decades, Sweden has been placed in the top five of the most sustainable countries in the world.

So this isn't a hard sell because Swedes have grown up with an intrinsic need to protect nature…naturally.

FOSTERING A SUSTAINABLE MIND

" Making simple changes in our everyday lives to save water or energy, cut waste or live more healthily can have huge benefits for people and the planet. Sustainable living isn't new. But with our busy lives, it isn't always easy. Most of us could use some help to live a more lagom lifestyle.
Joanna Yarrow, Head of Sustainable and Healthy Living, IKEA Group
"

Lagom awakens our consciousness and implores us to keep asking questions. It wants us to live with intention and an inquisitive mindfulness that keeps examining our actions, improving our lifestyles, and protecting what we cherish.

Many of us don't have the benefit of a system naturally designed to subconsciously foster a love for nature over time, like Swedes. Often, we don't live against a backdrop of policies that actively push us out our front doors to engage with and enjoy nature.

Despite this privilege, or lack thereof, we too want to make a difference when it comes to our environment. We want to do our part in preserving the rich natural resources that surround us. We want to be able to enjoy and tap into nature without harming or destroying it.

So how can you start developing our yown sustainable attitudes and what can lagom teach you about proactive green living?

Let's think of it like learning how to swim or learning a new language as an adult.

If you never had the opportunity to learn when you were a child, it's a lot harder once you're an adult but you push yourself to learn anyway. Acquiring these new skills may be challenging. You may fall many times along the way but the key is to dust yourself off and get back up again. So you need to learn new habits when it comes to developing your own sustainable way of thinking. And most of the time, capable teachers can show you the way.

In 2014 Swedish furniture and homeware giant IKEA launched its Live LAGOM project, in partnership with the University of Surrey's Centre for Environment and Sustainability and the non-profit organization Hubbub in the UK. Its mission is to bring this long-standing Swedish lifestyle practice of sustainability to the global masses. What started out as 200 IKEA coworkers receiving vouchers to invest in company products to help incorporate more sustainable habits into their homes turned into the Live LAGOM project for a wider audience.

The goal of the project is to show us all how small changes we make in our homes—from reducing water usage, to recycling and switching to LED light bulbs—can make a difference to the quality of our lives by saving us money and reducing our environmental footprints.

In essence, it shapes us into *lagomers*.

> **Who is a lagomer?**
>
> According to the IKEA Live LAGOM Project, a lagomer is a person who is working toward living a more lagom lifestyle—making small changes to their everyday life to minimize environmental impact, being thrifty with resources, and enjoying a fun, happy, and balanced life.
> **IKEA, Live LAGOM Project**

By promoting sustainable living as being attractive and affordable, little did IKEA know that it was inadvertently starting a worldwide movement introducing people to the wider virtues of lagom beyond tangible eco-practices.

It was giving us a glimpse into the Swedish secret of living well with contentment.

WASTE NOT, WANT NOT

We've probably all heard a form of the phrase "waste not, want not" at some point in our lives. Meaning, wastage is often the precursor to scarcity. The way we manage our resources lays the groundwork for either feast or famine in our lives.

We already know that lagom campaigns against waste in our lives. It wants us to reduce our consumption, be conscious about how much we use, and make sure we leave enough for others as well.

When it comes to living lagom, a lot of the actions surrounding building sustainable lifestyles are very practical and tangible. There are many concrete steps you can take—both small and big—to start making a difference in your life as well as within your community.

You can easily reduce the amount of energy you consume by turning off lights and appliances you aren't actively using, something which can make a huge difference. Not only do you save on your electricity bills, but you also do your small part in reducing energy use within your neighborhood, city, country, and subsequently, the larger world.

Regarding food, there are many campaigns around the world urging us to eat "ugly" food, meaning, perfectly fine fruits and vegetables that may not look exactly the way we want them to. Buying organic and sustainably grown or produced food can also make a cumulative impact. You can start being more mindful about companies that are environmentally and socially conscious in their operations.

Portion control, taking only what you know you can finish, reduces the amount of foods you toss into the bin. You can always donate canned items to local food banks and leftover produce to local food kitchens.

An occasional spring cleaning does a lot of good. Not only will it help you declutter, but it will help you identify items you can either sell or donate instead of throwing away.

Most Swedes don't grow their own food so lagom doesn't stipulate growing herbs, flowers, and vegetables on your balcony or in your garden, but this is another way of living sustainably if you naturally love or would like to try gardening. Growing your own produce will not only save you money, but also help replenish your supplies in ways you can adequately manage. You can grab a few sprigs of dill or leaves of mint and use just what you need instead of buying bunches that will end up going to waste.

Nothing replaces the rejuvenation we feel from soaking in a warm bubble bath after a long stressful day. Lagom definitely supports us spoiling ourselves by consciously taking care of our bodies and well-being. However, it also wants us to be mindful of the amount of resources we use while indulging—in this case, our water usage. So a small, sustainable step would be to cut down on the frequency of your baths and replace some of them with showers. This small gesture goes a long way in battling water shortage around the world. The same can also be said of turning off the taps while you brush our teeth.

To reduce waste in your life, lagom evaluates the environmental impact of your current lifestyle.

The three Rs—
REUSE, REFILL, RECYCLE

To encourage sustainable practices in your home, workplace, and community, you can begin by asking yourself if an item is reusable, refillable, or recyclable before you purchase it or throw it away. This line of reasoning will guide the way you interact with things you already own or choose to buy.

Many stores and supermarkets are already charging for plastic and paper bags in an effort to reduce environmental waste, encouraging us to reuse the ones we already have. This is a simple change we can all make in our daily lives.

The Swedish government has looked into cutting value-added taxes (VAT) on repair services in an effort to continually curb wasteful attitudes and promote the maintenance of everything from bicycles to home appliances.

Refillable containers can help rein in waste that comes from buying new packages every single time. This includes reusable bottles in lieu of plastic bottles and storage jars and spice bottles to consolidate and save. These small-scale efforts have a snowball effect when it comes to living green.

Paper, metal, rubber, and plastic can be reused to create new products—everything from packaging to even shoes—so recycling them helps the process and reduces the amount of natural resources we use. The same goes for upcycling, which means repurposing existing items and giving them new lives. These could be simple, creative projects such as saving boxes for arts and crafts or repainting that well-worn side table and moving it somewhere else in your home.

Remembering these three actions—reuse, refill, recycle—and keeping them in the back of your mind as your mantra for sustainability can help shape your behaviors in small yet powerful ways. This virtue is passed on to your children because they do what you do, not what you say.

THE FOOTPRINTS WE LEAVE BEHIND

Did you know Sweden has run out of rubbish?

The country's recycling process is so successful that less than 4% of waste is sent to landfills, and Sweden imports thousands of tons of rubbish from other European countries to keep its recycling plants up and running.

This feat wasn't achieved through government policies alone. It was accomplished by people like you and me—everyday folk—seeing the bigger picture of how our small actions impact the greater good. It all started with daily baby steps people were willing to make in their own lives to contribute to a more sustainable world around them.

If you change your way of looking at the Earth and its resources and think of those reserves as loans you borrow from your children, then the need for sustainable practices becomes obvious.

ECO LIVING TIPS

🌿 While you love a relaxing bath after a long, stressful day, you can also be more mindful about how many times you take them. More showers and fewer baths save a lot of water.

🌿 Use the dishwasher to bulk-wash dishes instead of hand-washing them to conserve water.

🌿 Turn off lights and unplug appliances that are not in use.

🌿 Recycle as much as you can, as often as you can. Those empty cans, bottles, and packages can be used to create new products.

🌿 Use refillable bottles rather than disposable ones.

🌿 Buy reusable bags so you avoid picking up plastic bags every time you go shopping.

🌿 Switch to energy-saving LED lights throughout your home. They use 80% less energy and last much longer.

🌿 Try hanging your clothes to dry in the sun instead of tumble drying. An extra plus in addition to saving energy, you'll get that fresh breezy scent only true sunshine gives.

🌿 Buying rechargeable batteries will save you more money in the long run and will stop wastage.

- Learn how to upcycle items instead of immediately throwing them away. Even those empty toilet rolls can be made into a fun creative project with kids.

- Wash your clothes at 40 degrees instead of 60 when possible—it cuts energy use in half.

- Set your refrigerator and freezer to the right temperatures to save energy.

- Lowering your indoor temperature by just one degree saves 5% on energy use.

- Consider growing your own food. You don't need a lot of space to grown herbs, for example. A sunny windowsill or balcony will do.

- Take the extra time to sell or donate unwanted clothes, furniture, and other items instead of tossing them.

- Look for simple ways you can reduce your carbon footprint by buying energy-efficient appliances, tools, and cars. Consider walking or biking, instead of driving, or even traveling by train rather than airplane.

LAGOM IN A CHANGING WORLD

LAGOM IS BEST... OR IS IT?

We're all gradually becoming citizens of the world rather than seeing ourselves as just residents of a specific country or region. Our cultures and traditions are beginning to morph, mold, and evolve alongside this new world order.

We embrace certain aspects of other people's culture to improve upon our lifestyles, and we refrain from cultural philosophies that seem unattainable or in direct contrast to our own long-held beliefs. We're constantly creating the ideal life we want by picking and choosing elements to adopt from other cultures. In addition to personal reflection and self-fulfillment, we constantly try to surround ourselves with the best lessons we've learned from others.

Lagom does the same because it doesn't exist in an idyllic bubble, blissfully disconnected from everyone else. It tries to find its footing in a world that is rapidly becoming globalized.

Espousing only the virtues of lagom and its original intent for our lives without talking about how lagom is navigating a changing world would provide a one-sided, unbalanced view of both its past and its future.

As we've explored in Chapter 1, on lagom in the context of culture and emotion, more negative connotations linked to words such as "mediocre," "average," and "middle of the road" have attached themselves to lagom, even though that word was originally meant to enrich our lives by managing our expectations and balancing our views.

Lagom is an overarching way of seeing, doing, and existing. It doesn't refer to specific moments of coziness and intimacy like the Danish hygge ethos does. It is the underpinning mentality of what it means to think like a Swede. It continually prunes the gardens of our lives, trimming out excess branches, and weeding out superfluous undergrowth. It leaves us with the highest-quality essentials we truly need and reduces stress in our lives. Yet this positive recalibration in our lives is often perceived as being risk-averse.

Even Sweden's tongue-in-cheek moniker—Land of Mellanmjölk—has negative connotations. If someone is referred to as a mellanmjölk person, they are often seen as uninspiring, mediocre, and rather boring.

So it's no surprise that many younger Swedes are trying to rid themselves of the stereotypes lagom brings with it. Once our needs are comfortably met—a privilege in itself—what about our wants?

Aren't we allowed to passionately pursue them too without caring what the world thinks?

"
In print: *Lagom* magazine

We take the concept of "lagom" as a starting point for the topics we cover in *Lagom* magazine by addressing the work-life balance in the lives of creative entrepreneurs and small business owners.

We want to inspire people by telling the stories of those who have set out on their own in order to pursue their own passions. Lagom the concept and *Lagom* the magazine both fit into the world's wider conversations about sustainability, globalization, and the importance of leading a fulfilled life.

Elliot & Samantha Stocks, editors, *Lagom* magazine
"

ON THE PURSUIT OF HAPPINESS

Once our self-confidence and sense of worth has been solidified, where do we naturally go from there?

The pinnacle of where we want to be is self-actualization. This means we want to visibly live out our authentic selves, share our talents with the world, and fully step into our personalities. This also means reassessing how lagom wants us to interact with each other and within our groups and communities. We're beginning to redefine what "appropriate" is when we apply lagom within our social and business contexts. Our bubbles of personal comfort are expanding and are unapologetically encroaching into the space of others.

Lagom seems to be fighting a losing battle against a world run by the instant gratification of social media, where we all want to be seen and heard, where it takes a matter of seconds to grab our attention or lose it, where the one who speaks the loudest is rewarded regardless of true talent.

Swedes themselves are reflecting upon lagom as their guiding spirit and many have grown weary of the restriction it brings. They too want to show the world their talent with pride and not restraint. Swedish celebrities are breaking out of that shell and living as unabashedly as they want to. Sports superstars like Zlatan Ibrahimović are anything but lagom on the field. Popstars such as Zara Larsson are as feisty as they come.

In our pursuit of happiness, lagom is embracing success, wealth, and fame with arms wide open, while firmly elbowing Cousin Jante out of the way.

The *2017 World Happiness Report* put Sweden in an enviable tenth place. According to the report, "increasingly, happiness is considered to be the proper measure of social progress and the goal of public policy.'"

The happiness index takes factors such as "caring, freedom, generosity, honesty, health, income, and good governance" into account when measuring just how happy the citizens of a country are. While tenth is clearly a respectable position to be in, Sweden finds itself behind its Scandinavian neighbors Norway (first place), Denmark (second place), and Iceland (third place). So it may seem that lagom is doing a lot of soul-searching right now.

ON CREATIVITY AND INNOVATION

" Approaching a complex design system with lots of functionality and intricacy, lagom has helped me make sense of complexity by seeking ruthlessly to promote harmony, balance, order, and keeping things "understated" when at all possible.

Jonathan Simcoe, senior designer and photographer

"

If an aversion to risk quenches creativity, then why is Sweden—which fundamentally runs on lagom—consistently one of the most innovative countries in the world?

It has a strong start-up scene which produced companies such as Skype and Spotify as well as a fierce gaming industry which birthed Minecraft, among others. Millionaires, tech gurus, and venture capitalists are remaking and reshaping the socio-economic mix within the country. While the gap between rich and poor is relatively small compared to other countries, it still exists and is slowly inching wider every year.

Swedish ingenuity stems from the fact that whatever they invest in to adequately meet their needs should last. It should be sustainable and it should be visually pleasing if they have to stare at it every day.

Think about some of your favorite Swedish products. We often revel in their simplicity, practicality, and understated beauty.

Lagom's relaxed yet direct approach to business continues to fuel these innovative industries. Its quest for simplicity has helped the tech industry whittle down complexity into intuitive artificial intelligence.

Lagom was never meant to represent middle of the road, mediocre, or average. It was meant to push us to operate at our most ideal levels in all aspects of life, focusing on our strengths, delegating our weaknesses, and seeking harmony and balance in the solutions we find.

THE POWER OF ACKNOWLEDGMENT

As social animals, we need each other.

We need tightly woven communities and strong support systems around us. We feel happy when we have satisfying relationships—close friends, family, colleagues—in our lives. This interdependence lets us know we aren't completely alone. A warm smile or kind gesture from a stranger can lift our spirits for the rest of the day.

If mindfulness is lagom's greatest virtue, then lack of acknowledgment is its deepest weakness. Born from the need not to inconvenience others by taking too much or talking too much, lagom has unwittingly built tight walls around its inner circles that are very hard to penetrate.

As humans, we naturally crave feedback and recognition. We want to be told we're doing a great job, that we're on track, that our ideas are outstanding. We want to be acknowledged. To be seen. To have our smiles and greetings returned, and to feel like we're part of one big, happy family.

While lagom fosters self-sufficiency and an active consideration for its neighbors by keeping its distance, the downside is that it also breeds deep loneliness in which one can begin to lose a sense of community. This is why many Swedes are slowly shedding lagom's demureness and lack of adequate appreciation, and are stepping boldly out of its shadow.

For newcomers to Sweden, trying to decipher the Silence of the Swedes can be very challenging, mostly because it can be very difficult to distinguish which ethos—lagom or jante—is at play after sharing personal accomplishments. Lagom at work wants us to keep our boasting to a minimum so we can continually keep expectations at a manageable level. Cousin Jante on its back says we shouldn't think and act like we're better than others.

For newcomers, who often have to show their professional cards and accolades as a way of gaining respect, meeting these unspoken rules can come with quite the culture shock.

According to the government agency Statistiska Centralbyrån, nearly one in five residents of Sweden has a foreign background. We bring with us different cultural beliefs and traditions, and we learn to live alongside these and adopt elements of lagom into our own lives.

Lagom's propensity for fairness and equality means opening its arms wide to receive those among us who are fleeing hardship and difficulty. Yet its natural avoidance of stressful situations and uncomfortable discussions creates a perceived insularity. This means integration, immigration, and diversity continue to be very heated, painful debates in the most open society, run by the most private people.

EXTREMES AS A NECESSITY FOR BALANCE

If lagom strives for balance, then aren't extremes in our lives part of that equation?

If we're always trimming the edges of our lives—not too much, not too little—then aren't we settling for the straightest path of least resistance with no risks?

If I want to gorge on takeaway food today and balance that out with a light salad tomorrow, am I not living lagom on some level?

This is the problem that arises when we keep equating lagom with the words "average" or "middle."

"Do not judge all you see, do not believe all you hear, do not do all you can, do not say all you know, do not eat all you have, let no one know what you have in your heart or in your wallet."

Swedish Proverb

Because at its core, lagom means optimal. It signifies the ideal state for each one of us where we feel the most content and happy in our lives. And it actively wants to push us closer to that medium.

If balancing crazy adventures around the world with lazy Sunday afternoons curled up indoors with a book makes me happy, then lagom says I need to be taking more crazy adventures and indulging in more lazy afternoons.

It is important for us to remember that lagom is a shape-shifter. It can be quantitative and qualitative. Tangible and intangible. Lagom wants us to cut out quantitative extremes in our lives such as extra belongings and expenses. But when it comes to qualitative experiences that we need in our lives, such as emotional and physical satisfaction, lagom wants us to fully meet them.

Lagom doesn't want me to feel guilty for gorging on that greasy takeaway food. It has never been about austerity and deprivation.

What lagom wants me to do is be more mindful about my emotions, my body, and my well-being. It wants me to sate my cravings with moderation, rather than deprive them. It also wants me to actively weigh the impact of indulging those desires on other parts of my life. In essence, this means stepping back to assess if an action is a good idea at the moment or not.

And if I do decide that takeaway is a fabulous idea, then lagom wants me to balance out those extra calories with some exercise to return myself to my own perfect equilibrium.

Lagom sows seeds of contentment in various aspects of our lives and wants them to sprout into full blooms of happiness and satisfaction.

INVITING LAGOM INTO OUR LIVES

" He who is content is rich.

Lao Tzu, ancient Chinese philosopher and writer

"

The lure of chasing our desires and wants is a lot more seductive than meeting our basic needs. We often feel that by truly living out our passions and aggressively chasing after what we want in life, we will invite contentment into our lives.

But if we strip lagom down to its core, exposing just our basic needs and addressing them as fully as we can with the highest quality we can afford, then we are already setting the stage for contentment. By unchaining ourselves from clutter and excess, we're free to pursue those passions with intention while learning to live with less by being mindful.

That intricate marriage between mindfulness and intention is what has given birth to lagom.

As I've mentioned, in our quest for leading happy lives, we often draw inspiration and learn from other cultures, and there are so many lessons lagom can teach us. Above all, we get to choose which lessons we want to apply in our own lives.

Since my first encounter with lagom as the awkward elephant in the room, I too have adopted aspects of this unspoken ethos into my everyday living. I have blended my own vibrant background and culture, built on a strong sense of community, with portions of lagom that have resonated the most with me at this particular stage in my life.

So how have I personally invited lagom into my life?

I have become a better listener by speaking less and sharing only relevant information, yet I have balanced this with my own culture of warmly embracing strangers and fully acknowledging them.

I have ditched fad diets in lieu of a more balanced and healthier relationship with food. I now choose to eat within reason and in moderation. While this might slow down those weight-loss plans, I am operating within a happier, more manageable space.

Regarding well-being, I have learned to say no more often and more importantly, not feel guilty about it. I am also a lot more compassionate with myself. If I fail, I no longer feel the need to hop right back up immediately. I only get up when I'm fully ready and I take the time I need to look after myself.

Reducing my choices of the clothes I wear and the beauty products I use has relieved unnecessary, rather superficial stress.

While I've never been a natural hoarder, we only keep what we truly need or love in our home, and we are more mindful about what we bring in to join the rest.

Looking at my work life, when it comes to sharing accomplishments, I am learning the seductive art of measured revelation. I have fully embraced the cool constraint of lagom that says you don't have to wear your successes on your sleeve or show all your professional cards at once.

I now consciously take one extra step back when it comes to planning and decision-making. There is a lot to be said for preparedness over intuition in some situations, though both virtues have their time and place in our lives.

However, unlike lagom's typical reserve concerning constructive feedback and recognition, I try to acknowledge others when they do something well or meaningful as often as I can.

I do live well within my financial means, buying less but investing in high quality. I have also developed healthy saving habits.

Beyond the basic energy- and water-saving actions I take every day, the three Rs—reuse, refill, and recycle—are my friends. I reuse as much as I can, I always have a refillable water bottle on me, and recycling is an institution in our home.

I've been threading lagom's most attractive qualities into the rich, cultural fabric of my own life and I've firmly slammed my door in Cousin Jante's face.

Lagom doesn't hold all the answers. And in many ways, it is a luxury of thought that thrives against a backdrop where our basic needs are adequately met.

But what it does hold are the keys to free us from the grips of overt consumption. It shapes us into more mindful creatures in tune with our bodies and our needs. It sharpens our curiosity and consciousness, and it provokes questions that help us better assess what we choose to bring into our lives—be they material items or relationships.

It wants us to keep questioning, improving, and maintaining by asking ourselves the very simple question: What can I do to feel content and balanced today?

Once you've identified those core values and priorities in your life, lagom wants you to strap on your boots and do the hard work to get there with as little self-inflicted stress as possible.

While you don't need to force yourself to grow potted plants on your balcony, or bike everywhere you go to prove your commitment to sustainability, you can still make meaningful changes in your life by picking which elements of lagom speak to certain parts of your life. You can apply the virtues of lagom that make sense within whatever mental space you currently inhabit. You can let those small conscious changes pull you closer to that core balance, where the most important things in your life are as they should be because you take adequate time to tend to them and make them flourish. And if you truly let them grow, they become that blanket of comfort and contentment that blooms around us.

This truly is the Swedish secret to living well.

After all, if you've been unhappy for far too long, isn't it time to make a change?

ACKNOWLEDGMENTS

No man—or in this case, woman—is an island, and this book won't have come to life the way I dreamt it would without the support of my family, dear friends, colleagues, and professional network, both here in Sweden and abroad. You have welcomed me into your homes and your hearts, and for this, I am very grateful.

First, I'd like to thank my wonderful kids, and most especially, my husband, Urban. Besides being my love, my life partner, and best friend, he's also my informal Swedish teacher, sounding board, and reality checker in perfect complement to my doe-eyed idealism.

A special thank you to the following professionals and experts who generously shared insightful quotes for this book: Margareta Schildt Landgren, John Duxbury, Mary Jo Kreitzer, Karin Weman, Linn Blomberg, Philip Warkander, Monica Förster, Claesson Koivisto Rune, Joshua Fields Millburn, Julien S. Bourrelle, Tünde Schütt, David Wiles, Joanna Yarrow, Ingela Gabrielsson, Kjell A. Nordström, Elliot and Samantha Stocks, Julie Lindahl, and Jonathan Simcoe.

I would like to thank fabulous illustrator and designer Sinem Erkas for her creativity and beautiful interpretation of lagom across these pages.

And last, but certainly by no means least, I would like to thank my editor Grace Paul for not only approaching me with this exciting book project, but being supportive and understanding as we worked through it together.

Understanding lagom takes a village.

ABOUT THE AUTHOR

Having lived on three different continents—Africa, North America, and now Europe—for extended periods of time, Lola A. Åkerström is drawn to the complexities and nuances of culture and how they manifest themselves within relationships.

She holds a master's degree in information systems from the University of Maryland. Lola worked as a consultant and programmer for over a decade before following her dreams of becoming a travel writer and photographer, exploring various cultures through food, tradition, and lifestyle.

Today, she's an award-winning writer, speaker, and photographer, represented by National Geographic Creative. She regularly contributes to high-profile publications such as *AFAR*, the *BBC*, the *Guardian*, *Lonely Planet*, *Travel + Leisure,* and *National Geographic Travel.* For more information on her work, visit www.akinmade.com.

She has received photography and writing awards, including recognition from the Society of American Travel Writers and North American Travel Journalists Association, to name a few.

In addition, Lola is the editor of *Slow Travel Stockholm*, an online magazine dedicated to exploring Sweden's capital city in depth (www.slowtravelstockholm.com).

She lives in Stockholm with her husband and children, and blogs at www.lolaakinmade.com.

" There is beauty to be seen and enjoyed. There is light to be captured and displayed. There is life to be lived. And amidst all the chaos and tangle of life, there is something beautiful in finding lagom. Where everything has its right place. Stolen moments of rest and balance. Even a sense of peace.

Jonathan Simcoe, senior designer and photographer
"